OUR LADY OF JOY

CARLOS G. VALLÉS, S. J.

2004
GUJARAT SAHITYA PRAKASH
P. B. 70 ANAND, GUJARAT 388 001
INDIA.

ISBN : 81-87886-83-8

Price : Rs. 75.00; $ 7.00

Published by Fr K.T. Mathew, S. J., Gujarat Sahitya Prakash,
P. Box 70, Anand 388 001, India.
Laser-set and printed by S. Abril, S. J., Anand Press,
P. Box 95, Gamdi–Anand, 388 001, India.

CONTENTS

CONTENTS

CONTENTS

CONTENTS

THE ANGEL AND THE MAID

"Rejoice, full of grace."

This greeting opens our history, brings heaven close to earth, changes the path of wandering humankind, and illumines our own lives as we join in life's pilgrimage under the new light of the announced redemption. "Rejoice" is the first word of the "Good News" to us and to the world. It is greeting and blessing, smile and promise, congratulations and guarantee. Everything blissfully packed in the Angel's word that opens the dialogue with the Maid. "Rejoice, full of grace." Whatever comes after that will be marked with the sign of joy, as the first word marks the tone of all that is to come in word and melody and grace. "Rejoice" is an Angel's word, the first expression of his rehearsed message, the anticipated summary of all that is to come. A trembling of wings, a breeze from heaven, a whiteness of clouds. "Angel" means "messenger"; and the fundamental message of God, in which all past, present and future of history is contained, is "Rejoice!".

In that first word are already Bethlehem and Jerusalem, the Mount of the Beatitudes and the Sea of Galilee, the Cross and the Empty Tomb, the Coming of the Spirit and the Founding of the Church, and with them we too, Christians of all times, rejoicing with our Mother, who was the first to rejoice, and full from this moment with the gratitude and hope that begin in joy and end in glory. There will be still long ways to travel in pain and long nights to watch in expectancy, as life is not lived without suffering, and bliss is not achieved without trial; but the keynote that ushers in time as it will usher in eternity is the word of joy from the lips of the Angel that will preside over humankind's history and our own lives, and is sounding already in our ears that we may grow accustomed to its tune.

The Angel comes by surprise. Mary knew and believed and expected and prayed with all the people of Israel for the coming of the Messiah. But the certainty of the hope does not remove the surprise of the visit. God enjoys surprising us. He is infinite and eternal, his being is above our thinking, and his power is beyond our imagining. He is the master of times and places, he can lengthen promises and shorten appointments, he is always new and unexpected

2

among the routines and the repetitions of us humans.
His arrival is always a surprise, and the coming of his
Angel is always news. Even Mary is a little startled
at Angel's presence. She is startled because she
somehow foresees the greatness of what is to come
before she is actually told. And so she reflects and
ponders while the Angel watches her and waits. The
dialogue the whole of creation is waiting for since the
days of Paradise Lost is to take place in full serenity
of mind and peace of soul.

Mary is our mother, and this means that from this
very moment her life is to be figure and model of our
lives, her experiences are to be glimpses of our own
hopes, and the episodes of her life are to be an image
and a sketch of what our own efforts are trying to
achieve. The visit of the Angel, meant very specially
and definitively for her, is also a lesson for us and a
teaching for our own striving in the humility of our
lives.

Many are God's angels, and their fundamental
mission is always to announce God's will for us. The
great annunciation of Gabriel the Archangel to the
Virgin at Nazareth becomes also an event in our lives
in humble and repeated annunciations, modest but
definite, through which God goes on manifesting to
us his plans for our lives, calling us to commitment
and to service, and delicately waiting for our
acceptance. In our case there are no wings of angels,
no white presences, no spoken words, no outward

3

happenings and no liturgical celebrations, but there certainly is communication, assurance, a divine presence in the human heart and a clearly proffered invitation in the silence of the ultimate recesses of the soul.

Our happiness lies in recognising the visit of the angel. Each inspiration is an angel, and each good desire is an annunciation. Instants of grace between God and the soul, dawns of redemption in the depths of our conscience, glimpses of light in the darkness of human existence. It is not only the call to consecrated life or the closeness of two hearts towards the sacrament of human love that are visitations of the angel, but every thrill of joy, every loving look, every tender feeling, every gentle caress, every open smile, every good word, every song, every beauty in human faces, goodness in human hearts and humour in life, all these are also heavenly visitations along the course of our daily lives. Every gesture that touches our soul, quickens our pulse, opens our eyes, and draws us closer to our own lives is the presence of an angel that opens up new gospels in the personal history of our own redemption.

It is up to us to recognise the coming of the angel. Let him not pass us by. There is so much noise and so much hurry, and everything is so dull and so blurred and so confused that we miss the figure of the angel and are deaf to his voice between the dissonances of our crowded speech. The angel does

4

not impose his presence, does not force his way in, does not shout for attention. He respects our own freedom, and so he approaches us modestly, speaks gently, waits in silence... and goes away sad if we don't look at him, don't listen to him, don't notice his presence.

How many frustrated annunciations are there in our lives! How many angelic greetings lost in the tumult of our worries! We complain that things don't work, that life is always the same and that there are no surprises or hopes or dreams any more. There are no new paths in our lives because we are not looking for them, there are no new answers because we have no new questions, there is no aim because there is no start, there is no angel because we are not alive to his presence, his figure, his greeting. Grace passes us by and life remains dull. Without Annunciation there is no Gospel.

Maybe this first lesson our Mother teaches us at her very entrance into salvation history is the most practical and fundamental and permanent of all. That is, to pay attention to the coming of the angel, to be ready, to be prompt. To recognise the messenger, to stop life, to listen to his word. Everything will come from there. If we know how to stop for a moment, to listen, to grasp, to reflect, to answer to the always new and always surprising and always timely invitation, we'll enter the current of grace that will take us ahead in life towards all the new landscapes

5

that are waiting for us to discover them. Everything hangs on that first word. The greeting, the meeting, the blessing: "Rejoice!"

"Full of grace"

The Angel does not call Mary by her name. He does something far more interesting. He gives her a new name. He baptises her at the beginning of the dialogue. "Full of grace". That is her name, because that is her exclusive prerogative. She is "the one full of grace", "the graceful", "the one who is pleasing to the eyes of God", "the one on whom God rejoices". Here too, this first attribute contains in itself, in projection and prophecy, all that is to follow in reality and in fullness. God's loving regard rests on Mary, and the whole life and the whole history of Mary for her own glory and for the welfare of humankind will now follow from that single look. God has looked upon her and has been pleased with her, and his project of salvation and his plans for joy and redemption for all men and women are set in motion through that woman who will open for God the way into this world. "Full of grace" is a compliment, a word of praise, a flower, a poem on the lips of the Angel; it is the noble elegance of a heavenly knight errant, it is deep theology in its powerful meaning to be explored and in its permanent beauty to be enjoyed. The Angel had rehearsed his presentation well.

Here, too, we can take comfort in the thought

6

that what is said of our Mother somehow reaches us, her children, too. It reaches us because we rejoice at all the beautiful things that are said of her; and it reaches us because something of all those blessings will touch us too, as we draw close to her and know her and love her. We too are in some humble but real measure, "touched by grace", "favoured by God", "graceful", "privileged" in having Mary as our mother and in forming, with Jesus, one family with her. God looks also upon us with benevolence and fills us with his graces, calls us "his beloved sons and daughters" as he solemnly called Jesus, our brother and first and foremost Son of Mary, "his beloved Son" in whom he is well pleased.

The Angel's greeting to Mary is the gate to Christian optimism. There will be strife and there will be trials in this world because life is a path and there are thorns on it, but already in the midst of us is one who possesses in fullness the joy of grace, the promise of redemption, the guarantee of eternity, and we share in those blessings through our faith and our love. All that is already contained in the first words of the Angel: "Rejoice, full of grace".

THE FIRST QUESTION

"How will this happen?"

These are Mary's first words. The Angel has
explained God's plan, has announced to Mary her
maternity, has pronounced the name of Jesus and has
declared that to him belong David's throne and the
kingship over the house of Jacob. These are all
expressions of Hebrew tradition which every Israelite
venerated and understood. Mary has understood it all.
She knows she is to be the gate and the way for God's
redeeming plans over his chosen people, central figure
in the fulfilment of the Messianic hopes, chosen woman
among all the women of Israel to incarnate the dream
of being the mother of the Messiah in the Promised
Land. Mother of the Messiah. Joy and bliss, privilege
and honour, grace and responsibility. She was going to
be the woman whom "all generations will call blessed".

Everything had been carefully planned, foreseen, prepared and decided upon by God. She had only to agree to it, and God would take care of everything. One would also think that one is not to put questions to God or ask for explanations from him. He has seen to everything, knows all the details, and resolves all difficulties, and so one can leave the carrying out of all those plans in his hands; and not only can, but should do so as an expression of faith and a declaration of trust.

And yet, Mary asks questions. Her first word is a question. She wants to know before she answers. She does not rush, does not act blindly, does not lose her balance even with that surprising piece of news. She wants to know how that proposal fits in with her own condition, how God's plan will integrate with her own plan and determination, how the Son of the Most High will be the Son of the Virgin. And that is why she asks. Quite naturally, discreetly, delicately, and at the same time quite clearly and innocently, she frames her own question. She allows for a brief silence to follow the Angel's enthusiasm, lowers her eyes in devote reflection, looks up again in honest eye contact for her transparency and her trust, and asks the heavenly messenger her courageous question, "How will this happen, as I know no man?"

I feel a thrill of joy when I hear my Mother ask this question. This is the first surprise in her existence, the expression of her dignity, the revelation of her

9

personality. Mary thinks. Mary is intelligent. Mary is independent. Mary feels free in the most overwhelming moment in the history of the relationship of God with men and women on earth. Mary quiets down, finds herself, pauses before the glorious proposal of honour and greatness, renews her assumed responsibility and asks clearly for a necessary explanation. How will this happen?

I admire the good sense, the freedom, the clarity, the serenity, the courage of her unexpected question. Till that moment we knew nothing about Mary, we hadn't heard her voice, we hadn't been informed of any of her words or actions or thoughts. This is the first time we hear her speak, the first words we hear from her lips, the first revelation of her character and her soul. And this first revelation makes it clear already why she is God's chosen one, why she represents us all with supreme dignity, why she is model and image of all the best we ourselves want to-be. God, in the deep and redeeming mystery of his own action, is the Lord of everything, and at the same time respects and honours the freedom of the men and women he creates; and so Mary, fully conscious of the mystery and alive to its consequences, shows herself to be free and responsible, independent and respectful in her dealing with the divine majesty that seeks her consent.

She asks before agreeing, she seeks information before committing herself. There is no doubt or

10

suspicion or any kind of uneasiness in her question; there is simply, much to our joy and our instruction, serenity, responsibility, independence and clarity in full measure. Mary's first word is our first inkling into her human greatness in the fullness of the divine grace. We, her sons and daughters, will later give her the title "Seat of Wisdom". She fully deserves it.

The idea and the practice of dialogue between superiors and subjects when it is question of orders, planning, different attitudes, or even at times of opposition and censure of conflicting views, has come to be a relatively new proposition in ecclesiastical circles. I submit that it is not new. Dialogue with no less an authority than Yahweh himself was customary with Moses or Abraham, and in the New Testament, Mary initiates the dialogue with the Archangel of God, in all its clarity, freedom, honesty and responsibility. With all respect and with a touch of humour I would like to see a new title added to her sacred litany: "Our Lady of Dialogue".

This first attitude of Mary's makes me now reflect on myself. If I want to be her son I have to be like her, and so, when orders and teachings and commands and obligations reach me from the legitimate authorities who speak in the name of God, I must not show blind submission or instinctive acquiescence, but I first must, like my own Mother, think and reflect and consult my own conscience and awaken my sincerity, and perhaps even show then the need for explanations before

11

hastening to declare my acceptance. If she knew how to express her questionings even before the Angel who was coming directly from God, I also may, and even will be under moral obligation to question messages and to request explanations from the legitimate authorities when my conscience tells me that what they propose to me does not fit with what I responsibly feel and freely confess. And then I'll wait for the answer from the angel.

The Angel answered Mary with biblical expressions of deep meaning and direct understanding. "The Holy Spirit will come upon you, and the power of the Most High will overshadow you." These are familiar terms to Hebrew ears. The cloud of the glory of God that overshadows the Tabernacle in the desert as well as the Ark of the Covenant under the wings of the Cherubim, that fills the sacred Temple in the moments of its consecration with the reality of the divine presence, and rests on the Holy City as a sign of the dwelling of God with his people. The cloud that guided Israel in the desert with a golden glow at night and a column of white in the day. The cloud that is power and presence and majesty and company.

Mary knows all that, has lived all that in her Saturday prayers and in the readings at the synagogue, has repeated those passages in the psalms and has prayed them in faith and devotion. And now all that tradition of history and experience and theology and redemption converges on her, and she, in her humility and her faithfulness, knows herself to be Ark of the Covenant, Temple of the Living God, Holy City, Mother of the coming Messiah who will carry out all that the Power of the Most High has promised in blessing and prophecy to his people, and in it to the whole humankind when he will make the whole earth into a Promised Land.

Mary understands. Her own intelligence, that had made her notice possible discrepancies in the beginning, opens up now for her new perspectives of grace and divine power which she knew by faith and now accepts in gratitude. The Angel had prepared his message well, and his explanation has been sufficient with its language of centuries and its echoes of history. Mary, the Daughter of Israel, is going to be the Mother of the Messiah. The shadow of the power of the Most High will once again give forth its light.

It was on the date of the feast of the Annunciation when I myself was ordained a priest together with six other Jesuit companions in the locality of Anand, traditional centre of the Catholic Mission in the province of Gujarat. The ceremony took place in the open air to accommodate the large number of faithful that wanted to accompany us in the best moment of our lives. We took our places on a stage precariously made up of American tins of milk-powder tightly tied together that creaked ominously as we walked on them in the elaborate ritual of the solemn ceremony.

13

The bishop anointed our hands, handed over to us the chalice with the paten, blessed us with the prayer that made us into ministers of the altar, of the word, and of God's pardon, and placed in our hands for the first time the bread that was the Body of Christ, and which we, together with him, had consecrated in that our first joint Eucharist. Those were the times before the Council when holy communion was received directly on the communicant's tongue, and the communicants' hands never touched the consecrated host. That is why that moment had a special meaning in the life of a priest, fondly prayed for and looked forward to, when for the first time in his life human hands touched divine sacraments. With this liturgical thrill in our fingers we gave our first joint blessing to relatives, friends and all the faithful, and went back in silence to the room where we had put on the sacred vestments for the ceremony.

On reaching there, the companion by my side stood for a moment looking at his hands and said to himself in a low voice which I heard: "How can this be?" He was wondering how his own hands had come to be the instruments of the highest mystery human hands can approach. I had been precisely the one who had read the day's Gospel at the Mass, and that had been precisely the scene of the Annunciation, with Mary's question in it, and I was suddenly shaken by the parallel between Mary's question looking at the Angel and the new priest looking at his hands. "How

14

can this be?" And I answered, also in a low voice that only he who had put the question could hear: "The Holy Spirit will come upon you, and the power of the Most High will overshadow you." We looked at each other, and our eyes went wet. The Annunciation still goes on.

VIRGIN AND MOTHER

"I know no man."

My father St Ignatius was about to kill a Moor because he denied Mary's virginity. Ignatius had already been converted to a holy life in Loyola, but had not yet acquired the wisdom he would acquire in Manresa, and was still a knight errant on a humble mule on his way to Montserrat where he was going to keep vigil over his habit as a pilgrim, laying before Mary's image his sword and his dagger to enter his new life.

He believed it was his duty as a knight to kill the Moor who had insulted Mary, but he doubted in his first lights as a pilgrim whether he could legitimately kill anyone. In his doubt he trusted his mule, let the Moor overtake him at a crossroads with the understanding that if his own mule would take the same way as the Moor, he would kill him; while if she took the other way, he would let him go. The mule, which someone has called a worthy descendant of Balaam's wise she-ass, chose the other way and saved the Moor's life. Ignatius kept his conscience at peace while his love for Mary grew as he approached the Dark Virgin of Montserrat.

I also feel in myself something of the spirit of the errant knight when I think about Mary's virginity. I know well all the historical, biological, theological, and cultural objections that seem to be the fashion among some authors that doubt, diminish or simply reject Mary's virginity even from Catholic quarters. If I had a sword and a mule, the Moor was going to have a rough time. Not even Balaam's she-ass would save him. This does not mean that I don't value research and respect opinions, which on the contrary I appreciate and enjoy, and I hope to be able to show it along this book as I go on quoting studies and researches which I love to read; but it does mean that those anti-virginity scholars, for all their good will and their vast knowledge, seem to have lost sight of the fact that what they adduce as objections to Mary's virginity are in fact arguments in its favour. This may look a little daring on my part, and so I tackle the point with all humility and sincerity. The sword and the dagger have remained for ever before Our Lady of Montserrat.

The objectors to virginity tell us that it would be unheard of that a young woman in Israel at the beginning of the first century would think or desire or much less would promise virginity. I agree to that, but I draw from it the opposite conclusion. In spite of that cultural, social, and religious attitude against virginity, there is such an amount of evidence in the case of Mary's decision and preservation of her virginity in a whole unanimous tradition from the very first sources of Christian information that this very contrast establishes the reality of the unusual fact and the strength of a testimony which could not have been invented against all that current.

I don't want to be aggressive, but in all humility and respect I do want to express clearly what I feel, and it is the following: 1) In Mary's time virginity was unknown in Israel. 2) On the other hand, Mary's virginity is firmly established by the unanimity of Gospel tradition. 3) The fact that Mary's virginity comes out so strongly witnessed to against the common practice at the time shows precisely that the fact imposed itself by its own reality and the undeniable evidence upon a society in which it was not expected. I proceed now to work out these three steps.

That virginity was not a positive value in Israel is a well-known fact. The Hebrew woman had to become a mother to fulfil herself as a woman. It was her duty to have children, to perpetuate the people

18

of God against the rigours of the desert and the attacks of the enemy, and to aspire to the greatest blessing all women in the chosen people desired, that was to place themselves in the line of generation of the future Messiah and thus to be among his ancestors in history. That is why sterility was a curse, and virginity was rejected. I give here some texts on the matter.

Not to be able to marry is the greatest punishment God can give his people. "From the towns of Judah and the streets of Jerusalem I shall banish all sounds of joy and gladness, the voices of bridegroom and bride; for the whole land will become desert" (Jeremiah 7:34). Sterility is a woman's greatest opprobrium. "When Rachel found that she bore Jacob no children, she became jealous of her sister and complained to Jacob, 'Give me sons, or I shall die!'" (Genesis 30:1). Such too, was Hannah's tragedy, till she miraculously conceived Samuel: "When Elkanah sacrificed, he gave several shares of the meat to his wife Peninnah with all her sons and daughters; but to Hannah he gave only one share; the Lord had not granted her children, yet it was Hannah whom Elkanah loved. Hannah's rival also used to torment and humiliate her because she had no children. This happened year after year when they went up to the house of the Lord; her rival used to torment her, until she was in tears and would not eat (1 Samuel 1:4–7). Sterility was woman's greatest affliction in Israel till

19

Mary's own times, and this is why Elisabeth rejoiced when she conceived John the Baptist in her old age: "This is the Lord's doing; now at last he has shown me favour and taken away from me the disgrace of childlessness" (Luke 1:25).

The most tragic incident in the whole of Israel's history as a proof of the popular rejection of virginity is the story, almost pagan in its cruelty but biblical in its message, that the Book of Judges narrates in all its pathetic realism:

> Then the Spirit of the Lord came upon Jephthah, who passed through Gilead and Manasseh, by Mizpah of Gilead, and from Mizpah over to the Ammonites. Jephthah made this vow to the Lord: 'If you will deliver the Ammonites into my hands, then the first creature that comes out of the door of my house to meet me when I return from them safely shall be the Lord's; I shall offer that as a whole-offering.
>
> So Jephthah crossed over to attack the Ammonites, and the Lord delivered them into his hands. He routed them with very great slaughter all the way from Aroer to near Minnith, taking twenty towns, and as far as Abel-keramim. Thus Ammon was subdued by Israel.
>
> When Jephthah arrived home to Mizpah, it was his daughter who came out to meet him with tambourines and dancing. She was his only child;

apart from her he had neither son nor daughter. At the sight of her, he tore his clothes and said, 'Oh my daughter, you have broken my heart! Such calamity you have brought on me! I have made a vow to the Lord and I cannot go back on it.'

She replied, 'Father, since you have made a vow to the Lord, do to me as your vow demands, now that the Lord has avenged you on the Ammonites, your enemies. But, father, grant me this one favour: spare me for two months, that I may roam the hills with my companions and mourn that I must die a virgin.' 'Go,' he said, and he let her depart for two months. She went with her companions and mourned her virginity on the hills. At the end of two months she came back to her father, and he fulfilled the vow he had made; she died a virgin. It became a tradition that the daughters of Israel should go year by year and commemorate for four days the daughter of Jephthah the Gileadite (Judges 11:29–40).

What they lament is not so much her death as her virginity, and they clearly say so. To die without reaching marriage and motherhood, was to die twice. It is true that there are some exceptions to this in the history of Israel, but they are few and weak. There is no doubt that the first and legitimate and we could almost say obligatory aspiration of every young Israelite woman was to become a wife and a mother among the chosen people.

21

And that is why Mary's exceptional attitude and the overwhelming testimonies that vouch for it from the beginning have such undeniable force. The reality of Mary's virginity claims our definite acceptance precisely because it appears against all the cultural and religious background of her times. Nobody could have invented an attitude so contrary to the prevailing custom, and if anyone would have invented it, it would have found no credibility and would have disappeared by itself. And yet, the idea found total acceptance. Matthew is absolutely explicit about the point: "His mother Mary was betrothed to Joseph; before their marriage she found she was going to have a child through the Holy Spirit" (1:18). Mark calls Jesus "son of Mary" (6:3) in circumstances that suggest an exclusive relation between Jesus and Mary in his birth. Luke introduces Mary as a virgin (1:27), explains in delicate detail the virginal conception (35), and focuses the whole scene of the Annunciation on the dialogue that asks for an explanation and obtains it on this fundamental point. For a moment of suspense the whole expectation of heaven is hanging on Mary's response, and Mary's response is waiting to ensure that her virginity will be safeguarded. The power of the scene which ushers in the incarnation cannot be underestimated. We know that the evangelists sought information in sources and witnesses and traditions that originated in the facts themselves, and this gives a great weight of guarantee and credibility to the exceptional, and therefore even more real virginity of Mary.

22

Mary's virginity is the proper channel for the coming of Jesus' divinity. And Mary's virginity is also symbol and image of what our own attitude should be towards the coming of God into our lives with his messages, his inspirations, his grace and his sacraments. Openness, readiness, fidelity, totality. We belong to God, and he makes his way towards us in our personal incarnations throughout our life in the Spirit. This is how two women theologians express it:

Mary, in her pregnant virginity, is what humankind is called to be from the beginning of creation: temple and abode open and inviting in all readiness and fullness, like a blank page ready to receive the jottings of the Spirit and become 'a letter from Christ'. (2 Corinthians 3:3).

Yet, more that the biological fact, it is the biblical story itself that points out the theological way that, through the witness of the first Christian community, leads up to the faith in God the saviour. Mary's virginity underlines the right God has to communicate with his people, not only through words, but also through wordless gestures that lead his people to the understanding and realising of the salvation in sight. Just as God's gift to his people – Jesus – does not come through the bodily relationship of two human beings but through the Power of the Most High, so our salvation does not come from us, but it is a free gift that has to be accepted with humility and faith.

The barrenness of a virgin body in itself is a figure of the impotence of humankind to work out its own salvation without the grace of God. When people drift away from God, their history becomes a succession of failures, disappointments and sufferings. When people wake up and accept the workings of the Spirit, dead bones come to life, the desert flowers, the virgin conceives. Mary's virginity is, thus, a sign of God's sovereignty, which approaches us through grace and makes it possible for us to enter into the way to the Kingdom (María, mujer profética, by Ivone Gebarra and María Clara L. Bingmer, p. 120).

It is Christian women, no doubt, as the two writers of the last quotation, that can best understand and make us understand the meaning of virginity and maternity as a human experience and as a mystery of faith. Such was the old and holy woman who gave me the best insight in this matter I've received in all my life. I was very small at the time, and hardly understood the meaning of the words, and she was an aunt of my father's, very old by then, who lived alone in her long widowhood. She had married young, and her husband had died shortly after their marriage before they had any children. So she had been a wife, but had never been a mother, thus living out in her life the exactly opposite situation Our Lady lived in hers. That is why I was struck by her spontaneous commentary, which remained forever imprinted in my mind, when someone in a gathering of women spoke of Mary and emphasised her sacrifice and abnegation in her combining her virginity with her motherhood; that is, how she had forgone the pleasures of matrimony while undertaking the labours of maternity, thus getting the rough side of both situations. That is what some other woman in the gathering said with full pious and devout intention. But then my old aunt, who had seen things diferently in her life, reacted quickly and exclaimed with a tone of conviction that withstood any opposition: "Virgin and Mother! How lucky!"

The aunt knew it. She knew how a woman values virginity, which was no more hers, and values maternity, which she had not known either. For her this was a double loss. And the very mention of her, who, among all women, had put together what that holy and wise old woman knew to be the best in the life of a woman, made her exclaim with definite certainty and clear conviction: "Virgin and Mother! How lucky!"

Such luck had not been hers, but precisely for that she knew it to be the greatest blessing for a woman, and so the childless widow praised and envied the Virgin Mother for her unique bliss. Virginity is not only bodily integrity but pristine innocence, morning dew, dawn without dusk; and now it flowers directly in Mary into maternity, which is the fullness of woman, gift of life, fruit in season and an echo of creation itself. All that, made now reality in the Maid whom the Angel greeted. And my old aunt had understood it all. Her commentary was worth more than a whole theological treatise. And my child's mind kept intact the intimate memory so that I could remember it at this moment to strengthen the sacred truth with a woman's spontaneous evidence: "Virgin and Mother! How lucky!

THE FIRST CHRISTIAN

"Be it done unto me according to your word."

     Mary does not ask any more questions. Once she has clearly seen God's proposal and the way it is to be carried out, she accepts without conditions. She has asked what she had to ask, and now she leaves to God the carrying out of his plans for the world and for her. She does not pretend to know beforehand what is going to happen to her, what consequences the assent she now gives will have for the rest of her life; she does not even ask for instructions how she is to behave and what she has to do and in which way will subsequent orders be communicated to her. She trusts God fully and commits herself to her mission without stopping to find out what that will mean for her by way of joy or suffering. She knows by instinct that God does not like to be pressed for details. He likes total commitment and open generosity. No conditions, hesitations, vacillations. For God to act freely and fully he has to be left at liberty without any restriction, and this is what Mary does with her brief and definite answer. The Angel, back in heaven, can report that his mission has been accomplished. He brings Mary's unconditional yes that opens for God all the wide ways of his redemptive action. The great work can now begin.

"Be it done unto me." "Be it done." Even grammar can teach us the lessons of the Spirit. Mary's intelligence that shone in her first question, shines here again in the expression of her own commitment. She does not say, "Yes, I'll do whatever you tell me." She chooses her verbs and nurses her words. She says: "Be it done." She knows that the action comes from above, from the Power of the Most High, from the Spirit under whose shadow she will live for ever in loving refuge and in close co-operation.

Of course, she will have to think and to plan and to undertake and to decide all that her own and her Son's life will bring to her in growing complexity and delicate choices; but she knows and she declares from this moment that all that personal activity will at the same time be only God's presence made active in her, intimate collaboration of effort and grace, blessed effect of the Power of the Most High on the humility of his Maid. This attitude gives peace and truth, shows faith and ensures results, unites heaven's inspiration with earth's labour in a single action that saves and redeems. Be it done unto me, while I, in the humility of my being and the limitation of my strength, will go on discerning, accepting, deciding, and so helping to carry out God's plan in my own life for the good of all those that will be touched by it. This is the right attitude.

We usually express our decisions in the first person singular. I do, I think, I work, I achieve. Or again we personalise our losses. I doubt, I stumble, I fail. This underlining of the "I" is dangerous in its consequences. It may tend in practice to make us forget God's grace and plan out our life as though everything depended only on our effort and our willpower. This is an error as old as humankind and as contemporary as all of us, and from it derive many of our disappointments in the way of practising virtue, dealing with others and praying before God. We miss our balance and spoil our chances by stressing our part of the bargain, and all seems to go well for a while with our plans and our efforts. But our efforts fall short of our expectations, and soon we are drawn to despair. This can be dangerous.

We must, instead, learn how to combine our effort, which must always be there, with God's grace that works in us as it worked in Mary. The balance is in the "be it done unto me", combined with our resolution to keep doing our best. This secret union of effort and faith is the essence of the ways of God with us humans. We have to do and to let do. We

29

have to remove obstacles so that the grace of God may find its way, and then strive to correspond with our efforts to that inspiring grace. Receptiveness and readiness make up our salvation.

There is still a very important point to consider in Mary's short answer to the Angel. "Be it done unto me according to your word." The word. This expression has a special importance in Luke's context when at the beginning of his gospel he records the double visit of the Angel to Zechariah and to Mary. Mary does not say, "Be it done as you say, or according to God's will or God's plan," she says, "According to your word." And Zechariah is scolded for not having believed in "the word" of the Angel who announced him a child in his old age. Luke, all along his gospel, is going to give as a regular trait of Jesus' disciples the fact of "listening to the word and carrying it out"; and so here, at the beginning of his gospel, when he presents Mary as she who has first listened to and fulfilled God's "word", he is making of her the first Christian, the first to listen to the Gospel and fulfilling it, so that she becomes image and model, help and inspiration for all that Christians in all times are meant to be. This important point deserves dwelling a little on it.

The parable of the sower that appears in Matthew, Mark, and Luke, has a special ending in Luke with the mention of the "word" in this particular sense. It is as follows:

But the seed in good soil represents those who bring a good and honest heart to the hearing of the word, hold it fast, and by their perseverance yield a harvest. (8:15)

To hear the word and to hold it fast is the characteristic of the disciple who follows Christ attracted by the power of his "word". Again, in the scene in which Jesus' Mother and his relatives visit him while he is engaged in his public ministry, Luke likewise differs from Matthew and Mark in his approach, and throws a new light on the point that is for him the prime characteristic of the true disciple:

His mother and his brothers arrived but could not get to him for the crowd. He was told, 'Your mother and brothers are standing outside, and want to see you.' He replied, 'My mother and my brothers are those who hear the word of God and act upon it' (8:19–21).

The connection is obvious. The parable has prepared the family reunion. Luke is the chronicler of Jesus' childhood which he narrates in his gospel, as he is also the historian of the Church's infancy which he narrates in The Acts of the Apostles. And in the above-quoted passage he shows us that the proof and measure of our belonging to the Christian family of Jesus is "to hear the word of God and act upon it". Thus Mary, who was the first to listen and to follow that word since the visit of the Angel, is the first member in Jesus' spiritual family, as she is the first

31

member in his human family. She is from the start Mother and model of all believers who are called, like her, to listen to God's word and to put it into practice so that God's plans may be fulfilled and humankind's redemption be effected.

There is still more. Luke gives us another text, this one exclusively his as it does not appear in the other gospels, and in that text he again underlines the fact that Mary's real greatness consists in listening to the word and acting upon it; that is, in being the most distinguished Christian in the service of the word, which is what, according to Luke's repeated teaching, constitutes true discipleship for the followers of Jesus. Mary is the first among all of us who love Jesus, not only because she is his Mother, but because she was the one who first and foremost understood his word and kept it. This is the text:

> While he was speaking thus, a woman in the crowd called out, 'Happy the womb that carried you and the breasts that suckled you!' He rejoined, 'No, happy are those who hear the word of God and keep it' (11:27–28).

Here again we have the clear and definite contrast between Mary's undeniable blessing in her motherhood, and the even greater blessing of receiving and keeping the word; that is, following Jesus with total dedication. Mary is blessed because she gave birth to Jesus as his mother, and even more blessed because she offered him her faith and her life as a believer. She was the first believer in time and in intensity. The first servant of the Word.

One last touch, typical and exclusive of Luke, completes the picture of the Word into which he fits his whole gospel and his own conception of the following of Christ. In two near-by passages, after the adoration of the Magi and the shepherds at Jesus' birth, when Jesus' visit to Jerusalem at twelve with all the incidents it gives rise to is over, Luke repeats an almost identical expression which strikes us as being both intimate and meaningful, particularly at the moment of the infancy and adolescence of Jesus when it appears. Luke observes twice:

> Mary treasured up all these words and pondered over them in her heart (2:19).

> His mother treasured up all these words in her heart (2:51).

The phrase occurs twice in the same chapter. It brings out Luke's favourite teaching about keeping the word as the main characteristic of the Christian. Hearing and keeping the word is Mary's chief occupation since she first listened to the Angel, in the deep feelings that accompanied Jesus' birth and growth, and all through her life that makes her "Mother of all the faithful" in her submission to the word that consecrates our faith.

The Fathers of the Church gave Mary a title that consisted in a play of words by only changing a small

33

letter into a capital. "Keeper of the Word" of "Keeper of the word". She looked after Jesus in his tender years (Keeper of the Word) and she observed his divine precepts always (Keeper of the word). Both titles fit Mary, as she gave birth, nursed, and protected Jesus as an ever loving and devoted Mother, and as she also listened to him in his message and his doctrine and his Gospel, and carried out his teachings all her life in love and obedience.

In the Jesuit church in Lima (Peru, South America) I saw a picture I have not seen in any other part of the world – and I have travelled a good deal and seen many churches. It is a loveable sample of theological innocence and charming devotion in the live colours of its landscape and the contemplative faces of its figures. It represents the Baptism of Our Lady in the river Jordan at the hands of Jesus. John the Baptist looks on reverently from the shore together with a devout crowd with joined hands and tender looks, and while Jesus pours out from a shell the baptismal waters on Mary's head, the Holy Spirit hovers over her in the figure of a dove, and God the Father raises his hand in blessing from the high heavens and pronounces the words that circle his face in letters of gold: "This is my beloved Daughter; in her I am well pleased."

It is an exact replica of Jesus' baptism in the Jordan. I say its theology is a little naive, as the painter forgot that Mary, having been conceived without original sin, did not need the sacrament to remove it as we all need; but those were times when the saying "Outside the Church there is no salvation" was taken very seriously, and as baptism is the official entry into the Church, they wanted to make sure she would be properly certified. And then, and at a greater depth of thought, if Jesus in his supreme innocence had been baptised by John, why could not Mary be baptised by Jesus? Similarity in all possible things between Mary and her divine Son was the devout principle that surely inspired the painter, and so he gave us his picture. It is not the expression of a historical reality, but it beautifully gives us the fruit of a heartfelt devotion.

I draw a valid conclusion from the charming picture. Mary as the first Christian. The first to be baptised, to be made officially a member of the Church, a believer, a disciple, a daughter of the faith and a follower of Jesus. The first, not only in time but in dignity, in depth and in solidity, in commitment and in continuity till the end. The first to "hear and keep the word", which is, in Luke's inspired conception, the very definition of the Christian. That is what we all are called to be with the help of her example and her blessing.

YOUTHFUL IMPULSE

"Mary greeted Elisabeth."

Nobody has spoken better of Mary than Elisabeth.
Whatever books have been written – including this
one –, whatever sermons have been preached or
panegyrics have been pronounced, all of them well
thought and well researched and well worthy of Mary,
none of them approaches, in briefness, in depth, and
in totality the happy and spontaneous exclamation
with which Elisabeth answered Mary's greeting. The
scene is worthy of Luke in the context of his masterly
dealing with Jesus' infancy.

When Elisabeth heard Mary's greeting, the baby
stirred in her womb. Then Elisabeth was filled with
the Holy Spirit and exclaimed in a loud voice,
'God's blessing is on you above all women, and
his blessing is on the fruit of your womb. Who

am I, that the mother of my Lord should visit me? I tell you, when your greeting sounded in my ears, the baby in my womb leapt for joy. Happy is she who has had faith that the Lord's promise to her would be fulfilled!' (Luke 1:41–45).

Elisabeth feels herself and her son to be filled with the Holy Spirit at the mere presence of Mary and the sound of her voice in her ears; she calls her "blessed among women", thus weaving the rosary that will sing Mary's glory in all languages, all ages, and all countries; proclaims her "Mother of the Lord" before councils and popes would do so, and praises her faith in God's word as the deep and firm root from where all these blessings spring forth and blossom out in Mary. Nobody can say more or better in so few words.

Elisabeth's inspiration comes from the presence of Mary. And that is a beautiful figure and image of what Mary does when she enters into our own lives. Mary, in her family visit with hurried step towards those with whom she can share the good news, brings with herself joy, brings the Holy Spirit, and brings faith. In the measure in which Mary comes to form part of our lives in memory and in prayer, in love and in trust, in intelligent study and in filial devotion, we experience the fullness of the Spirit, the joy of faith, the spontaneous inspiration to see God's marvels in ourselves and in all people with the generous outburst of evangelical joy.

37

Mary, wherever she goes, brings Jesus with her, and with him she brings grace and joy to all those who receive her in their homes. Her feminine touch, her readiness to travel, her affection towards her relatives, her youthful optimism, her beautiful face that will fill us with joy the day we see it, her singing voice that caused the child to dance with joy in his mother's womb, her spontaneous laughter that filled the whole house, all that is the most beautiful image known to our love and venerated by our faith. Of all the Gospel scenes in which Mary appears, this is my favourite one as a happy picture, meaningful beauty, contagious joy, irresistible charm, unhampered conversation, extended stay, and shared faith. Mary in her splendid youth, in her preserved virginity and her initial pregnancy, in her traveller's zest and her prompt service, in her charm and her familiarity is the most beautiful picture of the most beautiful of the daughters of the human race, of her that is for ever blessed among all women.

Elisabeth's words sounded both familiar and extraordinary in Mary's ears. They were extraordinary, as a woman had never held the exalted position Mary now held between the Old and the New Covenant, opening sacred history and inaugurating the redemption. And they were familiar too, because they reminded her of expressions the whole people of Israel treasured in its long pilgrimage through painful captivities towards the Promised Land. When Judith liberated the city of Betulia from Holophernes's threat, the city's chief, Ozias, addressed her in thankfulness and joy:

> Daughter, the blessing of God Most High rests on you more than on any other woman on earth; praise be to the Lord God who created heaven and earth; under his guidance you struck off the head of the leader of our enemies. As long as men commemorate the power of God, the sure hope which inspired you will never fade from their minds. May God make your deed redound to your honour for ever, and may he shower blessings on you! You risked your life for our nation when it was faced with humiliation. Boldly you went to meet the disaster that threatened us, and firmly you held to God's straight road. All the people responded, "Amen, Amen" (Judith 18:20).

Mary knew well the Scriptures, and she knew that Judith had been proclaimed blessed among women because God had entrusted to her the main role in an episode of the history of salvation of his people, and as such she was a sign and a figure of God's action through women and men for the good of all. And now Mary saw herself in the line of those celebrated women of the chosen people at the moment when the hopes of the coming of the Messiah were accomplished and the final liberation gave fullness and meaning to all the partial liberations that had preceded it.

"Blessed is the fruit of your womb" also calls to Mary's mind echoes of Moses' blessing when he proclaimed the Law of God to his people:

If you faithfully obey the Lord your God by diligently observing all his commandments which I lay on you this day, then the Lord your God will raise you high above all nations of the earth, and the following blessings will all come and light on you because you obey the Lord your God. A blessing on the fruit of your body40 (Deuteronomy 28:1–4).

Listening to the word of God, as Mary always did in her life and particularly so since her conversation with the Angel, carries with itself the blessing of fertility and fecundity in the seed that yields its fruit, be it in the parable of the sower or in the virgin birth, as all these are hidden signs and mystical parallels in the sacred books if we know how to read them with worshipful imagination.

Elisabeth also tells Mary: "How can the Mother of my Lord come to me?" And David had asked in his time: "How can the Ark of the Lord come to me?" (2 Samuel 6:9). I have already hinted how Mary, who had been "overshadowed by the Power of the Most High", is prefigured in the Ark of the Covenant under the shadow of the wings of the Cherubim (Exodus 25:20; 2 Chronicles 28:18). John in his gospel, quoting all these old familiar images, will say that "The Word was made flesh and pitched his tent among us" (1:14).

40

All these images and these traditions converge on Mary and make her into the sacred Ark of the New Covenant on whom the power of God has descended to dwell among us. It is a joy to hear these two women saying such beautiful things to each other, woman to woman, enjoying together their mutual bliss, and summing up at the same time in their quotations the whole history of which they knew themselves to be heirs and characters in that blessed moment in the annals of the people of God. Listening to them, one does not know whether one is listening to a chatting between friendly neighbours, or to a lecture on sacred scripture. And there still remains for us to see Mary's part in this inspired dialogue.

All this happy and joyful episode appears to me to be a thoughtful adventure on the part of the young woman full of life that Mary was, and who as such embarks on the sudden journey, enjoys her innocent freedom before going to her husband's house, talks freely with one she knows understands her, enjoys herself with her relatives, attends to Elisabeth in her delivery as preparation to her own when it comes, and so the girl that left home three months before returns to it now a mature woman. The Ark of the Covenant, by the way, remained also three months in the house of his keeper, Obed-edom the Gittite. Blessed three months.

OUR LADY OF JOY

"My soul tells out the greatness of the Lord."

All modern biblical scholars are agreed that Our Lady's song, the *Magnificat,* was not composed personally by Mary, not even by Luke, but that it comes from the first Judeo-Christian community as a sacred canticle or a liturgical song composed with anonymous fervour for community use as poetical and rhythmical expression of the first faith and the first cult in the primitive Church. This, at first sight, may disappoint us a little, used as we were to listen to the *Magnificat* from Mary's lips, to hear her exultant voice in each verse, to recite by heart the whole inspired poem, to sing aloud in the divine office's Vespers its haunting melody, always thinking of Mary as the origin of each word, listening to her accents in each verse, almost feeling we were reciting her own composition, her canticle, her literary masterpiece. On a first impression we feel a slight disappointment at the opinion of the experts, which seems to lower the strength and the charm of one of the most beautiful and intimate texts in the personal life of any lover of the gospels. We feel a little sad about that.

But a second impression corrects the first. Those same scholars – to whom in passing I want to express my gratitude for the good times they have given me in my life with their treatises and their teachings in the matters I love most and enjoy more deeply as is the study of the Bible – tell us that, precisely because it comes from the first Christian community, the *Magnificat* shows the great appreciation in which those first Christians held Mary, and the refined understanding they had reached of the truths of our faith and of our basic traditions which led them to express their feelings, their hopes and their beliefs so truly that the family composition that resulted from such faith and such love could well have come from the lips of Mary herself.

This is very important. It means that giving to Mary a privileged place in our love and in our cult is not a late growth of uncertain fervours, nor an uncouth exaggeration of reactionary Catholics. It is nothing of the kind. Mary's first faithful devotees, those who composed in her honour and placed on her lips the most exalted canticle of her humility and her greatness, were the very first believers in the Gospel, the first generation of Christians, the spontaneous witnesses of the direct faith that lived, conceived and expressed the mystery of our redemption in feeling and in words. They, before all else, recognised the exceptional role Mary played in the divine plan with her maternity, her personality, her dedication and her faith as example and encouragement to all those that would follow the new "way" as the first Christians liked to call Christianity (Acts of the Apostles 9:2, 18:25–26, 19:9,23, 22:4, 24:14,22); and gave shape in the unique canticle to all the love, the admiration, the devotion they felt for Mary since then; and then they passed that priceless heritage on to us with a joy and hope we now want to prove ourselves worthy of. The *Magnificat* is not only Mary's personal canticle, which it certainly is in her feelings and her joy and her faith, but it is also the tender and poetical expression of what the first Christians felt in their first and transparent understanding of God's redemptive action with his people. Therein lies its value and its beauty.

> My soul tells out the greatness of the Lord,
> my spirit rejoices in God my Saviour;
> for he has looked with favour on his servant,
> lowly as she is.

> From this day forward
> all generations will count me blessed,
> for the Mighty God has done great things for me.

44

His name is holy,
his mercy sure from generation to generation
toward those who fear him.

He has shown the might of his arm,
he has routed the proud and all their schemes;
he has brought down monarchs from their
thrones,
and raised on high the lowly.
He has filled the hungry with good things,
and sent the rich away empty.

He has come to the help of Israel his servant,
as he promised to our forefathers;
he has not forgotten to show mercy
to Abraham and his children's children
for ever
(Luke 1:46-55).

The song's keynote is joy. Mary is bursting with
it in every word and gesture and in her very voice.
She wants the whole world to know how happy she
is in that magnificent moment of promise and
prophecy, of blessings and grace, of youth and
maturity, with the whole history of Israel behind her
and all the future of humankind in front of her, with
the living character of that story beating life and joy
within her with all the tenderness of a son towards
his mother in the most intimate union on earth. It is
joy that opens Mary's lips; and all that comes after
that first outpouring is just the unveiling and
developing of the first overwhelming emotion.

To come closer to Mary we must enter into her joy. It is true that in Mary's own life there will be days of sorrow and moments of acute suffering as an essential part of her life. But the general atmosphere of her life with Joseph and Jesus, the tone of her youth, the ring of her voice, the shine in her eyes and the spring in her step all speak of joy and happiness and satisfaction in the Lord for all that he had done to her and to his people. Mary wants that all generations may call her blessed, not afflicted or sorrowful, and that we may rejoice with her for all the marvels God has worked in her. Her days of joy were many more than her hours of sorrow, and that is what her own words reflect.

The image the *Magnificat* gives us is that of a joyful and enthusiastic young woman, full of zest for life in all that she knew and had lived and was to live in the closeness of the most blessed presence on earth; and that is the authentic image of the Maid of Nazareth, of the chosen one of God and of our own dearest Mother. I'm afraid we have not always lived up to that joy, and our iconography contains many more sorrowful images of Mary than joyful ones. We are familiar with the image of her heart pierced through with seven swords than with her loving face beaming with joy. If we want to picture to ourselves the image of Mary as she sings her canticle before Elisabeth, we must dare and picture her smile, see her face open up, her eyes shine, her hands go up, and

46

her voice resound as her joy comes out from her soul through her body into her whole being and the whole surroundings that watch her. Joy is the constant of Mary's life, and, apart from her last sufferings close to the sufferings of her Son, that is the attitude that defines her best as it should define us if we want to be like her. If we want to be Mary's true sons and daughters, we must always be joyful.

"My spirit rejoices in God my Saviour."

CONTRAST OF SALVATION

"He has raised on high the lowly"

Mary's joy is not a selfish joy. She rejoices, of course, at the great things the power of God has worked in her, but that is because she sees in them a sign and a promise of the even greater things God has done and will do for his people "from generation to generation", and specially so for the humble and the oppressed. Mary's *Magnificat* is based on the contrast between the rich and powerful on one side, and the humble and needy on the other. And here, too, we see the essence of the Gospel prefigured and proclaimed beforehand in Mary's prophetic canticle.

Among the four evangelists, Luke is the one who brings out more the presence of the oppressed in

Jesus' ministry, and we notice at once the importance he gives to women, widows, sinners, and poor people, whom the society of the day considered as low and treated as outcasts. Luke underlines, and even dramatises what has been called "the inversion policy", that is, the fall of the mighty and the exaltation of the humble as a characteristic feature of the establishing of God's kingdom on earth. We all know those passages, but it is instructive to collect some of them and see their combined strength in the context of Luke's gospel.

First, the parable of the foolish rich man who planned to build bigger and bigger barns to store his crops and then "to take life easy, eat, drink and enjoy himself," and who is told "this very night you must surrender your life," and suddenly loses all that he had hoarded all along. "That is how it is with the man who piles up treasure for himself and remains a pauper in the sight of God" (12:16–21).

Then, the parable of the guests at the banquet, where the first have to yield their places to the last, since "everybody who exalts himself will be humbled; and whoever humbles himself will be exalted" (14:7–11).

The contrast between the proud rich man and Lazarus the beggar also ends up in an interchange of roles. "One day the poor man died and was carried away by the angels to be with Abraham. The rich man also died and was buried. In Hades, where he was in

49

torment, he looked up and there, far away, was Abraham with Lazarus close beside him" (16:19-31).

This same contrast and inversion of roles opens in Luke's gospel the Sermon on the Mount with his characteristic version of the Beatitudes where, instead of the eight Matthew gives, Luke mentions four blessings and four lamentations, bringing out once more dramatically the sharp contrast between the downtrodden who triumph at the end and the mighty ones who sink in their shame.

> Blessed are you who are in need;
> the kingdom of God is yours.
> Blessed are you who now go hungry;
> **you** will be satisfied.
> **Blessed** are you who weep now;
> you will laugh.

> Blessed are you when people hate you and ostracise you,
> when they insult you and slander your very name because of the Son of Man.
> On that day exult and dance for joy,
> for you have a rich reward in heaven;
> that is how their fathers treated the prophets.

> But alas for you who are rich;
> **you** have had your time of happiness.
> Alas for you who are well fed now;
> you will go hungry.
> Alas for you who laugh now;

50

you will mourn and weep.
Alas for you when all speak well of you;
that is how their fathers treated the false prophets
(6:20–26).

Mary's *Magnificat* acquires even a greater importance after these typical texts of Luke's gospel, as this inversion of roles, central to that gospel, is announced already in Mary's canticle, so that Mary turns out to be the first to proclaim in advance the doctrine that Jesus will repeatedly establish and insist upon all along his own ministry. Mary's *Magnificat* is thus the worthy gateway to Jesus' Gospel.

He has brought down monarchs from their thrones,
and raised on high the lowly.
He has filled the hungry with good things,
and sent the rich away empty
(1:52–53).

We are happily waking up to a new responsibility in these matters. Social consciousness, equal justice, the denouncing of oppression in all its forms, the shaking up of our consciences before the rampant inequality between classes in society, the friendship between all races and all countries, the dignity of all peoples and the unity of humankind, are now issues that are gaining acceptance and promising hope for our future on earth. In that noble endeavour we are encouraged when we realise that this commitment to justice and to liberation is the very heart of the Gospel, and the first thought of our common Mother.

Mother that she is, she worries first about those of her children that are most in need, and believer that she is, she sees in the uplifting of the poor a sign and a promise of God's power which, in the redemption of material captivity prefigures and announces the final redemption of spiritual captivity and the establishing of the Kingdom of God for ever. "If it is by the Spirit of God that I drive out the devils [devils of sickness and hunger, of tyranny and oppression, of violence and death], then be sure the Kingdom of God has already come upon you" (Matthew 12:28).

The *Magnificat* adds thus a new dimension to Mary's joy. She began by rejoicing when she saw and felt the marvels God had worked in her, and now she extends that joy to her glad feelings when she sees the wonders God enacts in others. This is no superficial rejoicing or passing feeling, but a deep joy at the workings of God in us, and, particularly, with the most humble, as she herself was, who in their own humility and suffering feel the strength of hope and the prophetic joy to know that God's justice will triumph over present injustice and will continue to do so till the final victory. This joy helps us in the fight for equality, purifying us from any ill-feeling or violence, and increasing our strength with its hope.

Mary's *Magnificat* has been sung in freedom struggles in our days as a community hymn, as a battle-cry and as a thanksgiving service in modern fronts of the fight for social justice. Nothing could give Mary a greater joy.

WOMAN TO WOMAN

"I announce to you a great joy."

The joy the angels announce is meant for the shepherds in the fields near Bethlehem, for Mary and Joseph by the side of the manger in the cave, and for all of us who share in the faith and the joy of the first Christmas. The centre of that joy is the young Mother cradling her Child in her arms and smiling at the little face of her newly born. What a joy to think that Jesus' joy reaches us reflected in Mary's face! There is more theology in that simple scene than in many pages of learned treatises. Jesus' birth is the object of contemplation rather than of dissertation. That is why I let now a Christian mother speak, when she, as a human mother herself, speaks of our common Mother with a woman's understanding and a mother's feeling. This is how Ornella Accatino speaks in her beautiful book, "A Mother Called Mary":

My children are now more or less Jesus' age, and so I can somehow imagine what went on between Jesus and Mary along all those thirty three years of loving intimacy. [She speaks with feminine delicacy and realism of the days when Mary prepared herself for the birth of the child, and then comes to the birth itself].

Mary did not cry, certainly did not cry when the miracle happened. She was alone at the end of the stable, sweating and panting. But she placed the child in her hands and took him near her face to look at him, to know him, to love that part of her that was now outside her. And she kissed him.

Who can describe the first kiss of a mother to her child? Who can spell out and reveal the bundle of feelings, emotions, blessedness and total commitment packed tight in that kiss? Such was Mary's first kiss to Jesus, sweet, slow, tender, passionate. Her lips caressed the wrinkled face, the little body that was being shaken by its first breathing, by the quick beating of the heart below the taut skin.

Nothing could now ever break that secret and strong link made up of love and anxiety, pride and trembling, faith and tenderness, that united mother and Son as it unites every mother with her son at birth, and remained for ever, stronger and stronger along life and death.

Did Mary think that that child was quite different from other children, that God had supernatural designs over him? I think that in those first moments, in her first experiences as a mother, Mary did not think of any great events. She just abandoned herself to the joy of those first contacts: she would look at Jesus' hands and wonder like any mother at the perfection of those tiny fingers, those brittle nails, surprisingly long, that she would pare with her teeth as any mother would do in any corner of the world. Then she combed with her hands his light hair, held firm the little head that turned on its fragile neck and observed the movement that rhythmically lifted and lowered the centre of his head, on top of his forehead [the fontanelle].

And Mary discovered also his voice, his child's voice. Weak and shapeless, that voice came from the throat of the child in the first instant after his birth, and filled all the corners of the stable. The ass and the ox turned slowly and sweetly their own large and hairy heads. That was the most beautiful voice in the world, the sound that was missing to make now the world perfect. Mary drank in that voice that filled her whole being. A little infant sigh is enough to bind love's link for ever (pp. 14–21).

56

This image of Mary listening to Jesus' voice is as touching as it must have been true. It was first the voice of a new-born child who expresses his desires in the first language he knows, namely crying, which is tender in its innocence and prophetic in its lamentation. Then that voice strengthened as the child grew and sharpened his vowels and learned new words and framed sentences and answered questions and began little by little to put questions himself, the questions of a growing child who wants to know everything while his parents answer him with readiness in the beginning, with patience later on, and finally even with annoyance as the child wants to know more than his parents ever knew and insists on asking.

Later came that marvellous moment in the development of a male child when he changes his voice, when nature makes him into an adolescent, when his throat broadens and settles, his vocal chords tune up, the soprano key turns into a baritone, and a new voice bears witness before society that a child has become a man. That was the voice in which Jesus would later proclaim the Beatitudes, would chat with his friends and would answer his judges; the voice of his last seven words on the cross and of his first greetings to his disciples after his resurrection. Mary was the first to hear that voice, and with it the tone, the accent, the conviction, the serenity, the depth, the melody and the charm that would accompany for life

57

him who was the Divine Word of the Father, and would express himself in human words before women and men.

Mary's joy that was announced by the Angel ("Rejoice, full of grace!"), stressed by the shepherds ("I announce to you a great joy"), and expressed in the vibrant melody of her canticle ("My spirit rejoices in God my Saviour"), passes now from Mother to Child day by day, look by look, smile by smile in the long nearness of thirty years which imprinted on the Son the features he had in advance imprinted on his Mother. He, who knew the physical and moral heritage that he would receive from his mother at the virgin conception, shapes her as he himself wants to be shaped in his bodily humanity. He gives to Mary the gift of joy because he wants to be joyful, and so they build together their home at Nazareth as a happy home for a happy family.

True, there were trials too and difficult moments and downright suffering. Simeon's prophecy, Jesus' staying back in Jerusalem at twelve, the death of Joseph, the continued poverty, the incomprehension of relatives and friends, the untold fear about what could at any moment happen and would certainly happen at the end... were all shadows that hovered over Nazareth, as similar shadows hover over all families on earth. But they were only passing shadows in fleeting moments, while there is no doubt that the greater part of those blessed thirty hears at Nazareth were times of joy between Mother and Son, of intimate bliss, happy closeness, blessedness that prefigured heaven's glory from earth. To think otherwise of Jesus and Mary would be to think mistakenly of the best Son and the best Mother, and to be unfair to the consoling fact of seeing the heavens' joy built into a family in an earthly home.

Ornella Accatino contemplates again, woman to woman, Jesus' infancy before Mary in the gospels:

> Jesus knows his daily prayers because Mary has repeated them with him every day. He has followed the Jewish rites and knows the meaning and the value of the Sabbath rest. He has learned to read, and follows with his finger on the parchment the sacred words of the Bible, and he even knows many parts by heart, as he has an extraordinary intelligence and memory.

> Mary watches him full of awe and of love. She lovingly takes up all household work, cleans, cooks, weaves. She grinds the grains of wheat between two stones in the small house mill and then binds the dough with water and leaven. The bread rises on the large wooden tray and then is baked in the oven. Mary has taken water from the well and has brought it home holding gracefully the earthen vessel on her steady head, and has seen to it that there was sufficient oil for the cooking and for the lamps.

Her lips have smiled again, her prayer has expressed itself in praising the Lord and thanking him. She is happy because she lives day by day close to those she loves, looking after Jesus from the faint dawn to the looming dusk, and during the nights full of stars (pp. 24–24).

Mary is happy, and Jesus with her. His home formation in intimate joy is the necessary preparation for his preaching, his own conviction, his eager sharing, the promise of joy for ever in heaven because he that proclaims it has lived it and felt it in the happy environment of his own family on earth.

THE EDGE OF THE SWORD

"They did not understand his answer."

Trouble begins. The child is growing, is a young adolescent, is finding himself, is beginning to put to himself the great questions of life all adolescents put to themselves, and to answer them with a depth and an insight no adolescent has ever answered them. And Mary feels the distance. And one day that distance in mind expresses itself in a distance on earth. Mary loses Jesus. She literally and painfully loses him on the way, in the city of a thousand streets and the sacred Temple; in the returning caravan of pilgrims, a full day on her way back with relatives and friends along the pilgrim path, she misses him. She had not yet realised that Jesus was by now having other interests and other preferences that were prompting him to a new behaviour and a new freedom that would entail some friction where till now all had been smoothness and bliss.

The momentary loss of visible contact between Mary and Jesus is symbol and image of the existential distance that, even in the midst of the family closeness, existed between both. Jesus, son of Mary, separates himself from his mother when he is only twelve years old, because he feels already the urge to define himself as the Only Son of the Father in his divine origin. And Mary deepens her own understanding and love for her Son who now becomes suddenly distant when he seemed to be more close.

The search took three days. Perhaps a figure of those three days the long wait between death and resurrection will take soon on a more painful and final occasion. Three days of agony and anguish, of darkness and uncertainty, of not understanding what had happened and not knowing what could happen now. Three days in which feelings deepened, concepts ripened, prophecies were recalled, prayers were prayed, and Mary came closer, in faith and mystery, to the Son that had gone away for a time, only to come back with a new light on his face and a new depth in his words. The Gospel leaves no doubt about the fact that Joseph and Mary did no understand Jesus' behaviour neither his explanation of it:

> His parents were astonished to see him there, and his mother said to him, 'My son, why have you treated us like this? Your father and I have been

anxiously searching for you.' 'Why did you search for me?' he said. 'Did you not know that I was bound to be in my Father's house?' But they did not understand what he meant (Luke 2:48–50).

But now the same evangelist that naively informs us of Mary's lack of understanding of the situation, adds at once the consideration that Mary kept reflecting on all this in order to reach a better understanding of it all.

Then he went back with them to Nazareth, and continued to be under their authority; his mother treasured up all these things in her heart. As Jesus grew he advanced in wisdom and in favour with God and men. (2:51–52)

If Jesus grew in wisdom, so did Mary with him, as she advanced, with her remembrance and her meditation, in the understanding and sensing the meaning of her Son's words and actions, seeing him more and more involved with the dreams that were taking shape in his mind, and which his Mother followed with respect and love while she tried to match Jesus' interior growth with her own. That was not easy, as simple appearances hid inner depths, and daily closeness covered up remote meanings. This was Mary's happiest task, as it was her continued trial in life. She had so see divine glimpses in familiar traits, and guess transcendent senses in spontaneous gestures. This daily practice required inner detachment and secret suffering, as she heard her Son speak words she did not understand, and, later, walk into sufferings that would also be her own.

Mary had been prepared for this life by the prophecy of a venerable old man who had taken the child Jesus in his arms when he was taken for the first time to the Temple to be offered to God, and who, after thanking God for that moment he had been expecting all his life with unfailing faith, turned to Mary and told her:

> This child is destined to be a sign that will be rejected; and a sword will pierce your own heart. Many in Israel will stand or fall because of him; and so the secret thoughts of many will be laid bare (Luke 2:34-35).

The sword that would pierce Mary to the heart has been traditionally interpreted as Mary's suffering at seeing Jesus suffer, particularly in his passion and death; and popular devotion has depicted in its images and expressed in its prayers seven swords that pierce the heart of the Mother of Sorrows at the passion of Jesus. This is very legitimate and very true, and yet that does not seem to be the direct meaning of those words of Simeon as the best biblical scholars interpret the image of the sword. They tell us that the sword signifies rather discernment, decision, separation between good and evil, between those who chose and are chosen for salvation and those who separate themselves from it and drift towards perdition. The sword pierces Mary, as it pierces all of us when it places us before the decision, that will mark us for eternity, to accept and confess in Jesus of Nazareth the Lord of our lives and of the whole creation in spite of his humble appearance and his death on the cross.

This was the trial of John the Baptist: "Are you the one who is to come, or shall we wait for someone else?" This is the trial of all of us, too, as we feel on our way through life the temptation of disappointment and discouragement when we find that our expectations do not always come true, that our prayers do not seem to be always heard, that we do not understand the ways of God and do not understand God himself; and doubts besiege us and we ask ourselves without actually framing the question, or lose heart without actually acknowledging it to ourselves; and the echoes of the Baptist's anguish sound deep in our hearts: "Was this what we were waiting for, is this the power of the resurrection that can change the world, is this Church truly the Bride of Christ, am I really a true Christian, a religious, a priest, and is my life what it ought to be with the strength of the sacraments and the grace of the Spirit; is it true that the Kingdom of God has arrived within us... or are we to wait for another interpretation or another occasion without knowing when or how this will be? Are you the one who is to come, or shall we wait for someone else?"

And this is, above all, the trial of Mary herself in her unshakeable faith and her unfailing love, but also in the hidden reality of her retired life, in the persisting mystery of the hidden presence, in the daily routine of the familiar dealings, in the hiding of the divinity and the painful darkness of Jesus' words she did not understand and Jesus' gestures she could not figure out in the trying solitude of her virginal maternity. It was not easy for Mary to understand her Son and assimilate and accept all that he was and did and meant in his days at Nazareth and in those of his outside activity farther and farther in place and in strangeness, through misunderstandings with relatives and with authorities, through rumours in the village and protests in the crowds, through condemnation in court and death on the cross. The sword of decision marked with its ruthless edge the whole of Mary's life and gave her the exalted merit and the unique greatness of being the one who answered with her unconditional commitment throughout her whole life that first revelation in faith and obedience, so that she was the first to believe and then the first to carry out to the end what has to be the personal answer of each believer in the following of Christ throughout their whole life and without any conditions.

Any person that comes into contact with the Gospel, is judged by his reaction to Jesus in his cultural context and his freedom of conscience. That is the way to combine those passages in which Jesus says that it is not for him to judge anybody ("God has not sent his Son into the world to judge the

66

world," John 3:17), with those in which he says that the Father has sent him precisely as a judge ("because he has entrusted all judgement to the Son", 5:22). The word "to judge" is the same in both passages in the original text, and that makes clear the idea of the judgement that Jesus represents. He does not judge by passing sentence from a law court, but by his own presence in history and in the soul, and by the reaction caused in each person by that presence. "No one who puts his faith in him comes under judgement; but the unbeliever has already been judged because he has not put his trust in God's only Son" (3:18). It is his presence, his message, his Gospel that "judges" the person who receives it or rejects it in theory or in practice; that is, it is rather the person that judges himself by his way of acting before the personal and intimate revelation of the Gospel in his circumstances, his context and his life. Each one "has already been judged" by his individual attitude before the private revelation of Jesus in his life. This is the sense of our call to the Gospel, our unavoidable responsibility, our most cherished hope. To answer, with God's grace, to the Gospel that is being announced to us, day by day and decision by decision. That is the sword that decides our salvation as it separates the generous answer from the cowardly refusal.

Mary is our model in this with her initial reaction to the Angel, and her continued response throughout her life in her sacred closeness to Jesus and in the painful tearing apart when the separation came. Mary had to suffer her relatives' misunderstanding, Jesus' silence, the anguish of her own forebodings, the pain of the parting, the hours of the passion, the agony of death, the solitude of years of waiting, the fading of old age. And her attitude was always exemplary, and her response grew clearer and stronger with every event. "Be it done unto me according to your word." Mary is model, inspiration and help for all of us in receiving God's word and acting up to it, in accepting Jesus with unshaken faith and with tender love, and in persevering to the end in the choice we had once made and always upheld as the one and only way that takes us to Jesus.

That was the sword Jesus himself said he had come to bring (Matthew 10:34), which means division, determination, discernment, separation as a challenge for each one of us and a settling of our way in life according to our decision, with God's grace, to follow his invitation or to be deaf to it. This is the supreme choice the people of Israel knew well and renewed in a body through their history ever since the celebrated occasion of the historic assembly of all the children of Israel in Shechem at the end of the conquest of the promised land:

Joshua assembled all the tribes of Israel at Shechem. He summoned the elders of Israel, the heads of families, the judges and officers. When they presented themselves before God, Joshua said to all the people:

'Hold the Lord in awe, and serve him in loyalty and truth. Put away the gods your fathers served beyond the Euphrates and in Egypt, and serve the Lord. But if it does not please you to serve the Lord, choose here and now whom you will serve; the gods whom your forefathers served beyond the Euphrates, or the gods of the Amorites in whose land you are living. But I and my family, we shall serve the Lord.'

The people answered, 'God forbid that we should forsake the Lord to serve other gods!' They declared: 'The Lord our God it was who brought us and our forefathers up from Egypt, that land of slavery; it was he who displayed those great signs before our eyes, who guarded us on all our wanderings among the many peoples through whose lands we passed. The Lord drove out before us the Amorites and all the peoples who lived in that country. We too shall serve the Lord; he is our God.'

So Joshua made a covenant for the people that day; he drew up a statute and an ordinance for them in Shechem and recorded its terms in the book of the law of God. He took a great stone and set it up there under the terebinth in the sanctuary of the Lord. He said to all the people, 'You see this stone – it will be a witness against us; for it has heard all the words which the Lord has spoken to us. If you renounce your God, it will be a witness against you.' Then Joshua dismissed the people, each man to his allotted holding (Joshua 24:1, 14–18, 25–28).

Mary, with her definitive choice, her standing perseverance, her total surrender and her fidelity through all trials, continues to be the first believer, the first servant of the Word, the loving Mother who shows us the way and guides our steps, and the Daughter of Israel who embodies in herself the surrender to the Lord that makes up his people and attains its fullness in the faith of the Daughter of Zion: "Blessed are you who have believed!" (Luke 1,45.)

FAMILY FEAST

"And the Mother of Jesus was there."

Weddings in the Orient are celebrated with song and with dance. It is not only the young that sing and dance at the tune of the band that compulsorily forms part of each wedding ceremony, but grown-ups and elders too, women and men, express their joy in open rhythm and graceful steps, keeping up the unbroken tradition of dancing the weddings of their sons and daughters and nieces and nephews and acquaintances and friends the dances they once danced at their own weddings. I know it, because I've had to dance at more than one wedding among families of friends in India where the dance is an essential part of the ceremony, and not taking part in it would be an offence to the bride and bridegroom and a blemish on the nuptial blessing which all the invitees invoke with their presence and their joy and their sharing in the ritual dances for the welfare of the newly-wed.

They are simple dances with easy to learn rhythmical steps in open circles, one for the women and one for the men, singing and answering the traditional rhymes of teasing and laughing in the happiest moment for two young people who start the adventure of their lives together. When I see the joy of the young couple at seeing me clumsily dancing in their circle I feel even happier than they feel, and wipe my perspiration as a tribute to the joy of two families. Let the music go on.

Mary danced in Cana of Galilee. Some of the wedding songs have to be sung by women, and they do it with their natural charm as a touch of colour and life in the traditional ceremony. It's a pity that no painter has thought of depicting Mary in her dance, that no poet has sung her gracefulness and her art and her joy in the wedding dances of the village in Galilee, that no theologian has delved into the joy and the meaning and the blessing and the promise expressed in those steps and turns and smiles and verses of the family feast. Artists and painters have painted for us the Sorrowful Mother, they have touched our hearts with her beautiful *Pietàs,* they have recited to us heartrending poems of her sufferings and her sorrows, and they have explained to us the mystery of pain and have consoled us in our own trials with the memory and the veneration of Mary

72

standing by the cross of Jesus, and all that is very good and very proper, and we need it all and it helps us and it has to be done and will be done; and those artists have also given us happy images of Our Lady in her glory with the risen Christ, in the Upper Room at the coming of the Holy Spirit, in her Ascension for her final and definitive joy in heaven, and all this is also good and essential fully to understand Mary, to live her life and to follow her example. But we also would have liked, and it would have helped us in our daily life and struggle, if they had also given us pictures and poems and theology and contemplation of the daily joys of Mary, her laughter with her neighbours, her singing on her way to and from the well, her dancing in the friendly wedding at Cana in Galilee. Something in Mary has escaped us till now. It is time to recover the full image of our Mother.

A wedding is joy in itself, and the very fact of attending it is a sharing in that joy, joining in the feast and celebrating life. One of the very few things we know from the gospels about Mary, and also narrated at full length, is precisely her going to another village to attend a wedding. This is quite a large part of the full picture the gospels give us of Mary, and it is telling us with its extension and proportion that this cheerfulness and this joy was an essential part of Mary's character, that she enjoyed feasts and communicated joy, that anyone would like to have her by the side in all moments of life because her presence brought joy and cheer to all those she met. Such a person was Mary. And Mary is our Mother.

If the mere fact of attending a wedding is a sign of joy, what we know about Mary's behaviour at the wedding enhances even more her mission to gladden all places and all persons touched by her presence. What Mary did at that wedding was to prevent its being spoiled, to prevent that the newly-weds and their parents and their families would lose face, to prevent joy from being lost. There was a moment of danger, there was a passing cloud over the celebrations in the highest moment of the wedding banquet, the whole feast was about to be wrecked, and the joy was about to turn into sadness. In the Orient, and I know that also by experience, the number of guests is not counted as exactly as it is done in the West. In the West the banquet takes place in a hotel, the tables and chairs have been counted, their number matches the number of guests who have announced their coming, and no guest lacks a chair, while few chairs, if any, remain empty. In the East we are not so exact. The invitations have been sent generously, an answer has been requested (R.S.V.P.), but everybody knows that many will not take the trouble to answer and yet they will come, while others may announce their coming and not turn up in the end. The figures remain hazy, calculations are only approximate and uncertain, and preparations have to be made for all eventualities.

The worry about food falling short becomes an obsession with the bride's parents – who are those who offer the banquet – as they plan for the event, which would turn into a fiasco if food would go short. That would be a disgrace for the whole family, and a very inauspicious beginning for the newly-weds – in a land where omens and portents are made much of. If the main dish, particularly the sweet dishes that are the highlights in the menu, would fall short in a notorious way, the whole feast would be ruined. I have seen a boy of the family shoot out suddenly towards the end of the meal to fetch hurriedly a similar sweet as the one in the menu from some nearby sweet-shop to cover up the fact that the main dish was over and so save the family's honour before the crisis was noticed. And in the days preceding the wedding I've heard many times the repeated warning from everybody to everybody, "We must take care the main sweet does not run out!"

At Cana it was the wine that ran out. And at that time and in that place the wine was even more important than the food. The wine was the measure of the host's good taste, the show of his wealth, the proof of his generosity. Good and abundant drink could even cover up an inferior menu. But nothing could hide or excuse or justify a deficiency in the wine. Quality and quantity. If at the given moment in the middle of the feast someone would proffer his empty glass for a refill and it would remain empty, the alarm would spread, telling looks would be interchanged, faces would wither and the feast would be literally ruined. This happened at Cana. Or it was about to happen. The feast was about to end in disgrace.

But someone saw it. Someone who had the sensitivity to notice things before anybody else would, who knew the importance of a good wine for a good feast, who did not want that a young couple would start their adventure in life on the wrong foot, who appreciated the good name of a family, the honour due to the guests and the joy of a wedding feast. And Mary intervened. And the feast was saved. And that is how we know that Mary loves feasts, loves to see them go well, loves to see all happy in them, to the extent that she is ready to do all she can – and she can do much – to make the feast a success. Mary saved the feast.

And there is still another joy theme in this detailed narrative of Mary's action. That is the wine itself. Anything else could have run short, or any other problem could have arisen, and Mary would have come to the rescue in any case, but the fact is that the issue was wine, and since in John, who narrates the episode, every word has a special meaning, every element is a sign, and every event is a prophecy, the wine too must be having its own special meaning here. And the meaning of wine is joy. The Hebrews knew that and they sang to the fruit of the vine in their liturgy and in their meetings. Psalm 103 exalts the glories of creation, and it orders the rains to come and ripen fruits to nourish and strengthen men and women on earth:

> From your dwelling you water the hills;
> the earth is enriched by your provision.
> You make grass grow for the cattle
> and plants for the use of mortals,
> producing grain from the earth,
> food to sustain their strength,
> wine to gladden the hearts of the people,
> and oil to make their faces shine
> (13–15).

And the Book of Ecclesiasticus proclaims the universal conviction of all primitive peoples:

> "Wine puts life into anyone
> who drinks it in moderation.
> What is life to somebody deprived of wine?
> Was it not created to gladden the heart?
> Wine brings gaiety and high spirits
> if people know when to drink and when to stop
> (31:27–28).

Mary helps in achieving that the object that "gladdens the heart" be not missing where she is, because she wants joy to be spread around her, and she does it with her presence, with her smile, and with her intervention when wine runs short. And the new wine, when it comes, turns out to be the best, as the catering-in-charge has to recognise when he tastes it and calls the host to tell him:

77

"Everyone else serves the best wine first, and the poorer only when the guests have drunk freely; but you have kept the best wine till now."

And the quantity too was generous:

There were six stone water-jars standing near, of the kind used for Jewish rites of purification; each held from twenty to thirty gallons.

That is a quantity that no wedding party could exhaust however much they drank. Symbol, again, of joy and abundance in the proceedings of the feast and in the vicissitudes of life. No fear of dearth, and no lowering down the standards of quality.

The image of the banquet will convert itself in Jesus' lips, through image and parable, into a prophecy of the Kingdom of God in which the ultimate joy will reign supreme: "Many will come from east and west to sit with Abraham, Isaac, and Jacob at the banquet in the Kingdom of Heaven" (Matthew 8:11). And this nuptial banquet at Cana, complete with the presence of Jesus and Mary in it, will stand as model and reference where all of Jesus' parables in his preachings will find their expression and their meaning. "The Kingdom of God is similar to a king who celebrated a wedding banquet for his son..." The Kingdom of God is similar to Cana in Galilee. And Mary was there.

By the way. Jesus danced too.

78

LET THE FEAST GO ON

"They have no wine left."

We are so used to these words of Mary's that they do not surprise us any more, though in themselves and at a first reading they are really surprising. "They have no wine left." According to John who narrates the scene for us, "So Jesus performed at Cana in Galilee the first of the signs which revealed his glory and led his disciples to believe in him" (John 2:11). That means that nobody, not even Mary herself, had seen him perform any miracle before. This was "the first of the signs." Later, Jesus would lay his hands on the sick, heal lepers with a word, calm storms and bring the dead back to life; but nothing of this had happened before Cana. When the news of Jesus' powers would later spread among all the people, crowds would come claiming attention for their ailments, as they knew he could do for them what he had done for others. But those voices had not yet been heard because those miracles had not yet taken place. It took someone, who did not need those testimonies of others because she had believed from the beginning, to inaugurate the series of petitions for grace and for help that others will later take up and will continue even in our days before him whose voice even the winds and the seas obeyed. "They have no wine left."

As simple as that. As though it were just obvious that the simple mention in passing of a concrete need was enough for Jesus to remedy it. And the fact is that for Mary it *was* obvious. "Blessed are you who have believed!", was what Elizabeth had said of her. But even before I highlight her faith, I notice her sensibility as a woman and as a mother. She had noticed, she had realised, she had perceived the lack of wine before any other, even before her own Son would, apparently, notice it. She had noticed that something was wrong, that there was a worry in the air, that the feast was in danger. Just a comment, a head turned, a worried look, a subdued exchange between two persons in a corner. The crisis has not yet broken into the open, but Mary has noticed it. Her feminine touch and her motherly care have alerted her before a situation that can bring pain to others.

This gentleness, this awareness, this promptness are wonderful traits of our Mother's character. Nobody has asked her to intervene, nobody expects her to act, since, as I've said just now, nobody knew they could ask a miracle from Jesus, and so it was meaningless to have recourse to Mary. But she has seen it, has felt it, and has acted upon it. Mary is our best help in heaven, because she knows our failings before we even realise them, and knows how to mention them quietly and discreetly to her Son for him to remedy them. With her in our midst, we can freely celebrate the feast. Wine will not be wanting.

Jesus' closest disciples, even after having seen him work wonders among sicknesses and storms, could not bring themselves to trust him to remedy extreme situations, and it did not occur to them to have recourse to him, not even when Jesus himself was hinting that he could certainly intervene. This happened at the multiplication of the loaves:

> Jesus called his disciples and said to them, 'My heart goes out to these people; they have been with me now for three days and have nothing to eat. I do not want to send them away hungry; they might faint on the way.' The disciples replied, 'Where in this remote place can we find bread enough to feed such a crowd?'
> (Matthew 15:32–33.)

They did not expect the miracle. They did not think of asking for it. They just take note of the situation, they regret to see the crowds go hungry, and they express their own helplessness not to be able to do anything to help. There is a way of saying, "They have no bread", which only tells of compassion and resignation; and there is a way of saying "They have no wine", that leads on to action by any means one can find within reach. This was Mary's way. She could mention the situation, draw the attention of her Son to it, speak and wait; and she does it with all the simplicity of her character and all the efficacy of her word. Her faith and her timely hint solved the problem.

There was somebody who did learn Mary's way of prayer by hinting. They were women too, who in their feminine sensibility speak with Mary's own accent, and it is John too who gave us Mary's words in Cana, the one who now gives us the words of the two sisters in their message from Bethany:

> There was a man named Lazarus who had fallen ill. His home was at Bethany, the village of Mary and her sister Martha. The sisters sent a message to Jesus: 'Sir, you should know that your friend lies ill' (11:1–3).

The same touch in the message, even though this time the urgency of the grave sickness is added, and it will result in death. But the parallel is perfect. "Your friend lies ill." "They have no wine." It is enough to mention the fact, to give the news, to speak and wait. It is enough that Jesus knows it, and that we know he knows it. It is enough to inform him in time, knowing as we do that this is not information since he already knows everything before he is told, but that it is a gentle prayer and a delicate representation to mention our interest in the matter and to leave it to him to do whatever he thinks best. This is the middle way between saying nothing and demanding an immediate solution. It is prayer which knows how to be discreet because there is full trust in him who hears the prayer and who knows what it is to be done. Keeping quiet never got anybody anywhere. The art is to know how to speak, how to say, how to mention something, and to know how to do it without imposition, without demand, without threats. This is the way of the trustful prayer, the close intimacy, the familiar faith. It is the most efficacious prayer, as it is the most innocent request.

It is also a courageous prayer. It takes pluck to do it, and to do it before others who watch. How did Mary imagine Jesus was going to react? How was he to remedy the situation? What solution would he find? Where would the wine come from? There was no precedent in the matter, this was no easy problem, it required and immediate and quiet solution before the lack of wine was noticed and the harm was done. But Mary did not worry about all this. It was for her just to say what she felt, and it was for Jesus to find a way out. The harder the problem, the closer it brings us to God. Faith does not recoil at difficulties, on the contrary, it grows on them and knows that the answer will always be far beyond anything it would itself be able to imagine. Let us leave it to him for whom it is enough to know our interests in order to act immediately for the good of all.

This is now for me, too, the best prayer I can make to Mary on any occasion, any need, and danger in my life, any desire of my heart. "Mother, I have no wine." She will smile, because she knows well where those words come from. And the feast will go on.

MOTHER AND WOMAN

"And what do I owe to you, woman?"

    However translators translate and interpreters interpret, these are hard words on the lips of Jesus. Jesus used the term "woman" when he addressed other women in conversation, and that was delicate and polite. Thus he addressed the Canaanite woman who asked for her daughter's healing in the confines of Tyre and Sidon (Matthew 15:28), the woman he made stand up straight (Luke 13:12), the Samaritan woman (John 4:21), Mary Magdalene after his resurrection (20:15). But in the whole of Hebrew and Greek literature, as known to specialists in the matter, there is not a single example of a son calling his mother "woman". The word surprises us, we could honestly say shocks us, when we hear it from the lips of Jesus in direct address to his Mother. And it shocks

us even more on the only other occasion in which
Jesus addressed again his Mother in the Gospel, that
is, on the cross while he entrusts her to his beloved
disciple: "Woman, there is your son" (John 19:26).
With reference to this last occasion, Ornella Accatino,
whom I quoted earlier, speaks out her mother's heart
and says:

> Yes, Jesus has been thoughtful to think of her, of
> her future life as a lonely widow, and has
> entrusted her to his youngest and most loved
> disciple. This has been a loving gesture. But why
> does he call her 'woman'? The term is too cold
> for us. Why doesn't he say, 'mother'? Is this not
> the word she was waiting for, longing for?

> I know all the interpretations biblical scholars give
> of these words of Jesus. He has meant to entrust
> the whole of humankind, in the person of John,
> to his mother. Yes, so it is. But if I feel myself in
> her place, I am not satisfied. The word she
> wanted to hear was 'Mother!'
> (p. 65).

The scholars' explanations are not without interest,
and they do help us in our desire for a better and
deeper understanding of every word in the Bible. They
remind us that the term "woman" is used in the Book
of Genesis for Eve, mother of all the living, and
contrasting figure to Mary, our Mother, so that in it
comes out the universality of Mary's maternity in the
spirit as was that of Eve's maternity in the flesh.

Christian Latin poets play on words with Eve's name, *EVA,* and the Angel's greeting to Mary, *AVE,* which is *EVA* inverted, thus meaning that Eve caused our ruin by her disobedience, while Mary effects our salvation by her obedience, one being the opposite of the other. Here is the Genesis text, which also strikes us as we remark that Eve is not given her proper name in the whole scene in Paradise, and it appears only at the end of the whole story:

> The man said, 'The woman you gave to be with me gave me fruit from the tree, and I ate it.' The Lord God said to the woman, 'What have you done?' The woman answered, 'It was the serpent who deceived me into eating it.' Then the Lord God said to the serpent:
> 'Because you have done this
> you are cursed alone of all cattle
> and the creatures of the wild.
> On your belly you will crawl,
> and dust you will eat
> all the days of your life.
> I shall put enmity between you and the woman,
> between your brood and hers.
> They will strike at your head,
> and you will strike at their heel.'
> To the woman he said:
> 'I shall give you great labour in childbearing;
> with labour you will bear children.

87

You will desire your husband,
but he will be your master.'

And to the man he said:
'Because you have listened to your wife
and have eaten from the tree which I forbade
you,
on your account the earth will be cursed.
You will get your food from it only by labour
all the days of your life;
It will yield thorns and thistles for you.
You will eat of the produce of the field,
and only by the sweat of your brow
will you win your bread
until you return to the earth;
for from it you were taken.
Dust you are, to dust you will return.'

The man named his wife Eve because she was
the mother of all living beings
(3:12–20).

Given that the first Christians were well
acquainted with the Genesis narrative, and that John
brings out in his gospel whatever it may be – a
symbol, an image or a sign of new realities in old
parallels – it is not unthinkable that the purposeful use
of the word "woman" in his gospel was meant to
remind us prophetically of the first woman whose
action when endangering the future of humankind was
a figure by contrast of Mary's action in setting things
right again for the human race.

Even so, the roughness of the word "woman" stands out even more in Jesus' lips as we listen to the words that follow, which in its most exact translation would be, "And what is there between you and me?" Here, too, scholars bring us parallel texts in Scripture to make the sense clear. An example: the Second Book of Kings, chapter three, tells how Jehoshaphat, king of Israel, went with the king of Edom to consult the prophet Elisha about a point that concerned them both, and, as a first reaction, the prophet refused to answer and told the king of Edom: "And what is there between you and me? Go rather to you father's prophets and to your mother's prophets!" But the king of Israel insisted, and Elisha asked for a minstrel who played to him, and he prophesised to his tunes. Here the phrase means, "What have I to do with you?" or "That is your problem, what do I care?" In any case, it shows an initial refusal, only to soften down at once and do what he has been asked.

The phrase, then, in Jesus' lips means simply that his point of view differed from that of his Mother's in the matter. He was thinking only of carrying our his Father's will, since, as he would later say, his only concern was "to do what pleases him" (John 8:29). And he knew that the Father's plans at the moment did not seem to contemplate the beginning of the signs and miracles that were to accompany his preaching later. That is why he takes his distance and says, "It is no concern of mine." This is the meaning.

89

Putting it in our roundabout way, it is as though Jesus were telling his Mother: "Look, I understand. You have a perfectly understandable interest in helping this family in every possible way, while my only concern is with my Father's will; and his will, as I understand it at the moment, does not foresee any special action of mine in these circumstances. Better let things be as they are." There is always the rough tone of the verbal expression, but at least we understand its meaning and lighten its weight.

To these theological and exegetical considerations we can add a simple psychological insight that, with all respect and reverence towards the best Son and the best Mother the world has seen, can also help us to understand the play of feelings that makes us human, as fully human were Jesus and Mary too. Every son, as he grows up, feels the need to assert himself against the influence his parents have exerted over him in his first years and even after those first years, with their points of view, their tastes, their customs, their attitudes and their whole way of thinking and acting in the family and in society, in work and in games, in conversation and in prayer. The parents have trained the child according to their own duty and their love, and always for his own good and the good of all; but a moment arrives, welcome and necessary on one side and painful and disconcerting on the other, in which the son wants to find himself as a person, feels he is a free and independent individual in his ideas and his actions, gets over the inherited weight of the traditions imposed upon him till then, and wants to be fully himself in his own identity, originality and liberty.

That moment in life arrived for Jesus too. For him Mary's influence had been even greater than that of other mothers over their sons, and that for two reasons: because Jesus descended from her alone in his birth, and because Joseph died early, for the gospels do not mention him after Nazareth. Mary's had been the greatest influence over Jesus during all those long years, and a blessed influence it was in the intimacy and the mystery that have been delicately veiled from our inquisitive eyes. But every influence calls, in its due time, for a reaction of independence. This happened in Jesus too, with all the more strength, as in him the reaction expressed his divine origin in the midst of human surroundings. He had to assert before his own parents that above all things "he had to mind his Father's business" as he had told them when he was only twelve.

This attitude, fully proper and wholesome, prompts Jesus to emphasise his own independence even before his Mother, and he does it in gesture and in word. He remains in Jerusalem as a boy, takes leave of Mary as a young man, declares, as his Mother approaches him, that his mother and his brothers are all those who do the will of God, and derives towards "those that hear the word of God and keep it" the praises a woman in the crowd had directed towards "the womb that bore you and the breasts that nursed you." And then he uses the word "woman" when addressing her. In all this there is no question of estrangement or fight or confrontation, but only of his clear and timely declaration of his independence from Mary as a mature person and as his Father's son. Mary was, without doubt, the first to understand that attitude. She knew she had given him the best she had, and she was glad to see he was now advancing further ahead from that position towards new horizons that he alone could reach. To be present with full reverence and wonder – and at times with suffering and pain too – at the growing up of her Son as a person and as a Messiah was always Mary's greatest joy as a woman and as a Mother.

AHEAD OF THE TIMES

"My hour has not yet come."

The hour. The hour of Jesus. The hour of the Father. Jesus' answer to Mary reveals to us here one of the concepts dearest to Jesus and essential to understand him and his work. It is enough to cast a glance over some of the texts in which the word is used, in order to understand its importance and gauge its depth:

To the Samaritan woman: "The hour is coming, indeed it is already here, when true worshippers will worship the Father in spirit and in truth" (John 4:23).

In the Temple: "At this they tried to seize him, but no one could lay hands on him because his hour had not yet come" (7:30).

To the Greek proselytes: "The hour has come for the Son of Man to be glorified" (12:23). "And what am I to say? Father, save me from this hour?" (27.)

To his disciples: "Still asleep? Still resting? The hour has come! The Son of Man is betrayed into the hands of sinners" (Matthew 26:45).

To the guards that come to seize him: "This is your hour – when darkness reigns" (Luke 22:53).

At the Last Supper: "Jesus knew that his hour had come and that he must leave this world and go to the Father" (John 13:1).

To the Father: "Father, the hour has come. Glorify your Son that the Son may glorify you (17:1).

The "hour", of which Jesus speaks to his Mother at Cana, is the plan fixed by the Father for the salvation of humankind, and, within it, for every action and every event calculated from eternity and made reality when its moment comes. This time is sacred, is known only by the Father, and, as Jesus himself said, "It is not for you to know the dates or times which the Father has set within his own control" (Acts 1:7). Again, "About that day and hour no one knows, not even the angels in heaven, not even the Son; no one but the Father alone" (Matthew 24:36). It is for Jesus to be alert, open, ready and obedient to the Father's will to discern the moment, feel in his own being, that is, one with the Father that the hour has come, and act then in the fullness of his commitment.

We find in the Bible a twin expression to the "hour", of deep meaning and repeated use in the history of salvation and in our own lives, which is "the fullness of time". Each event has its own time, and it happens under God's providence when that time arrives, when the count is full, when the waiting comes to an end, when the fruit ripens and nature blooms into spring. This happens in the great happenings that mark the history of humankind, as well as in the small incidents that make up our own lives. Everything has its moment, its time, its "fullness", and in our knowing, recognising, expecting, desiring, welcoming that fullness is the key to the fulfilment of history and to the new flowering of our own lives.

It is enough to open our ears to this expression as it is repeated in biblical contexts of salvation, in order to feel its importance and tune our souls to the expectation, the advent, the arriving and the fullness of God's action within his people, and through it into our own lives and into the whole of humankind for its future hopes and its final joy. We all are a humble part of that glorious fullness that angels announce and men and women carry out united in the hope of the God who calls all people of good will for the fulfilment of his plan of salvation for all. Versions of the Scriptures vary, but the expression "fullness of time" is the same beneath them all:

But when the fullness of time came, God sent his Son, born of a woman, born under the law, to buy freedom for those who were under the law, in order that we might attain the status of sons (Galatians 4:4).

The time has arrived; the Kingdom of God is upon you. Repent, and believe the gospel (Mark 1:15).

All these things that happened to them were symbolic, and were recorded as a warning for us, upon whom the fullness of the times has come (1 Corinthians 10:11).

He has made known to us his secret purpose, in accordance with the plan which he determined beforehand in Christ, to be put into effect when the fullness of time came: namely, that the universe, everything in heaven and on earth, might be brought into a unity in Christ (Ephesians 1:9-10).

Christ has appeared once for all at the fullness of time to abolish sin by the sacrifice of himself (Hebrews 9:26).

We now understand better the dialogue between Mother and Son. Mary sees the immediate need of the family in trouble, while Jesus waits for the sign that will tell him the moment, the time, the hour in which he is to act, here particularly the hour for the beginning of his public preaching with the strength of the Spirit and the witness of signs that will accompany and enhance his presence and his words. Jesus is waiting but the hour has not yet come, and faced with that situation he states his position and keeps his distance as it becomes him to do. His attitude is genuine and true, and Mary knows it.

But then Mary also knows something else, and we, too, know it with her. That is one of the most practical and most consoling truths of our faith. Mary knows it from the traditions of her people, from her prayers in the synagogue, and from her own experience; and we know it from the Scriptures and from tradition and from our own faith and experience. This consoling truth is that, although God has fixed the hour of his visitation in the great moments of redemption of his people and in its small moments of enlightening our lives, he does permit and wishes in his providence that we ask him to anticipate the time of his visitation, and he does it most willingly when we ask him.

This is the lovely play between grace and prayer, between the Father's desire to send us his Spirit and the heavenly protocol that we should ask him first to do so, between Advent and Christmas, between the hour fixed from the beginning of time and its anticipation granted to us today. Divine play that makes heaven rejoice and awakens the earth to the mutual collaboration of the fundamental desires that are eternal in their hope and actual in their realisation.

97

The faithful Hebrews's favourite prayer every Saturday in the synagogue was the prayer for the coming of the Messiah, and the conviction was firm among them that those prayers would bring forward the date of his coming. Isaiah's prayer was the most used by them, as it is also loved and used by us today:

Rain righteousness, you heavens,
let the skies above pour it down;
let the earth open for it
that the Saviour may appear
(45:8).

Jesus himself, when in his preaching he spoke of the hardships of the last times, said that the duration of that trial would be shorter than it had been previously foreseen, as a consideration in favour of the chosen ones: "If that time of troubles were not cut short, no living thing could survive; but for the sake of God's chosen it will be cut short" (Matthew 24:22).

Peter, in his great speech after healing the lame man who begged for alms at the Beautiful Gate at the ninth hour, exhorted all those who were listening to him to be converted and to accelerate with their holy desires the coming of the Lord, the second coming in glorious triumph to usher in the eternal kingdom for humankind, a coming that will take place all the earlier if we call for it in our prayers:

Repent, therefore, and turn to God, so that your

sins may be wiped out. Then the Lord may grant you a time of recovery and send the Messiah appointed for you, that is, Jesus. He must be received into heaven until the time comes for the universal restoration of which God has spoken through his holy prophets from the beginning (Acts 3:19–21).

The first Christians were looking forward to this second coming of Christ with growing impatience, and seeing that Jesus was not coming back as they expected, were disappointed and were losing hope. Peter's second letter has a revealing passage that reflects this impatience and answers it by asking the Christians to pray that their desire and their hope be made a reality as soon as possible, since their prayers can bring forward the date of Jesus' coming:

Look forward to the coming of the day of God, and work to hasten it on (3:12).

Our prayers can bring forward the coming of Christ, the moment of grace, the fulfilment of the plans of the Father, the climax of human history. This is the great lesson of the Scriptures, the consoling hope of the Christian faith, the timely and practical lesson of Mary's presence at Cana. Jesus declares that his hour has not yet come, and Mary goes ahead with her pleading as though the hour had already arrived. And the hour arrives. The clock of eternity is put forward, the time-tables are adjusted, the angels work quickly at their winged messages, and the fullness of time makes itself present in that little village in Galilee. The wedding guests smile with the new wine, the family breathes relief, Mary secretly enjoys her daring adventure, Jesus enters fully into his active life, and his disciples believe in him.

In our own little wants we'll do well to think of the experience at Cana and of her that knew how to bring forward the moment of grace with her faith and her request. In times of trials and doubts, of dryness and temptation, of waiting and struggling, of darkness and unease, we'll do well to take up the prayer that brings dates forward, shortens trials and accelerates graces. The hour can be brought forward. And Mary, our Mother, is the one who best knows how to do it.

THE FIRST SIGN

"Do whatever he tells you."

It has taken us a full chapter to approach the understanding of Jesus' words, and to uncover in them, not a refusal to act but an invitation to believe. It took Mary only one second to do that. Though, of course, she also had in her favour the fact that she could see Jesus' face, perceive his tone, guess his intention through his whole attitude of gesture and voice. She, through her long years of living with Jesus, through her woman's intuition and her mother's love, knew whatever Jesus thought in his heart even if his words sounded austere and forbidding. She guessed she could go ahead, did not recoil before the apparent refusal, turned to the servers in all naturalness and told them as though Jesus had already agreed to help: "Do whatever he tells you."

These words of Mary, too, awake biblical echoes. In Egypt, when the seven lean years foretold by Joseph set in, and people began to go hungry, they resorted to Pharaoh, and Pharaoh used those same words:

> When the famine came to be felt through all Egypt, the people appealed to Pharaoh for food and he ordered them: 'Go to Joseph and do whatever he tells you'
> (Genesis 41:55).

In the desert, at the foot of Mount Sinai, when Moses receives the law of God from his hands and comes down from the mountain to present it to the people, he gets this answer which is the basis of the whole history of Israel:

> Moses went and repeated to the people all the words of the Lord, all his laws. With one voice the whole people answered, 'We will do everything the Lord has told us'
> (Exodus 24:3).

And, closer still, Mary in a way is only quoting herself and telling others what she herself had practised as her main attitude in life. She had told the Angel, "May it be as you have said," and now she tells others to do just the same, "Do whatever he tells you." Mary had a right to tell others to do whatever they were told to do in God's name, because that was what she herself had done in the first place and what had made her be all she was and stand where she stood. When the strength of a whole life backs the sense of a word, the word becomes credible and elicits assent. "Do whatever he tells you."

Always in the Bible, and even more in John's gospel, each word has eternal echoes, and we do well to read actual meanings in ancient expressions, and in taking as told to us what in similar circumstances was told to others. That is why we can and we should take these words, among the very few of Mary's words that have been recorded for us, as addressed to us with maternal care, and see in them her best advice to us and the best directive for our own lives. "Do whatever he tells you." To listen, to pay attention, to receive the message, to understand its meaning; and then, simply and directly, to carry out what we have been told. Loving obedience, ready awareness, joyful execution. Even if what we are told to do seems as useless as filling up with water "six stone water-jars, of the kind used for Jewish rites of purification, each holding from twenty to thirty gallons." The water-jars may yield excellent wine, and the rite of purification may turn into an unexpected toast at a wedding.

The ritual purification represents the Law of Moses. "For Pharisees and Jews in general never eat without washing their hands, in obedience to ancient tradition; and on coming from the market-place they never eat without first washing. And there are many other points on which they maintain traditional rules, for example in the washing of cups and jugs and copper bowls" (Mark 7:3–4). The image of the waters of purification giving way to the wine at a banquet is quite a lesson in John's theology. The Law of Moses gives way to the Gospel, the legal contract gives way to free grace, Sinai gives way to Golgotha, and so "he who is to come" in the person of Jesus as Messiah fulfils all that old images and ancient prophecies in the long history of Israel had prefigured and foretold.

This is the new people of God, made now into a Church, in legitimate succession to the first people in Israel. It is "the fullness of time" that has at last arrived after long marches and battles and deserts and rivers. It is the Promised Land, not any more in an earthly land of finite frontiers, but in spirit and truth in the spaces of grace that encompass all men and women of good will in all ages to be and to come. The Kingdom of God has arrived.

All this happened in Cana of Galilee "on the third day" after the encounter of Jesus with Philip and Nathanael which the same John relates at the end of the previous chapter. And the mention of "the third day" cannot remain without its own mystery in the theological insight and the mystical feeling that characterise the gospel of John. The third day is the space of time required for the preparation of the people before the presence of God in the solemn pact at the Sinai, the sacred waiting between the announcement of the meeting and the proclamation of the Ten Commandments, the keen expectation for the revelation of the glory of God and the sealing of the Covenant that forms the people of God for its new history.

> When Moses reported to the Lord the pledge given by the people, the Lord said to him, 'Go to the people and hallow them today and tomorrow and have them wash their clothes. They must be ready by the third day, because on that day the Lord will descend on Mount Sinai in the sight of all the people (Exodus 19:9–11).

On the third day, too, Jesus's death on the cross gave way to the morning of the resurrection, as he himself had foretold in John's own gospel: "Destroy this Temple and in three days I will raise it up again. The temple he was speaking of was his body" (2:19-21). The two women writers, Ivone Gebarra and Maria Clara L. Bingemer, whom I have already quoted, in a book that is delicately feminine and deeply theological, *María, mujer profética* ("Mary, Woman of Prophecy"), comment thus the significance of "the third day":

> The episode of Cana sets itself, thus, as a parallel in retrospect to the event at Sinai, under the new light of the incarnation of God himself, the new law in time and in the history of humankind; and also as a parallel in prophecy to the paschal era that will fully manifest the resurrection. The sign of Cana occurs in the context of a wedding feast in which God's covenant with humankind is

105

celebrated, the covenant that was initiated at Sinai and will find its summit at Easter (p. 91).

The sign of Cana, the first of the seven that John relates in his gospel, thus acquires a special importance, as it goes far beyond being just a gesture of timely help to a friendly family, and becomes figure, prophecy, pledge and celebration of the redeeming action of God with his people. This was the importance of the sign, and of Mary with it.

SILENCE THAT SPEAKS

"Jesus went down to Capernaum with his mother."

After Cana, Mary speaks no more in the gospels. And there are no more words of Jesus addressed to her, till the cross. This is a long gap that surprises us a little, as we would like to know a little more of our Mother, would like to have more words from her for our comfort and our guidance. Though we have also learned how to respect her silence, to appreciate its meaning and to understand its secret, since we know she keeps all things in her heart, and can obtain a miracle with a simple request.

Theologians who specialise in the mystery of Mary have also their own explanations of this gap of information about her, following the idea we have already seen that Luke presents Mary as the first believer in the Gospel and the first disciple of Christ since she "listened to the word of God and kept it", which is the sign and definition of the true believer. Their considerations, based as they are on serious research and devout contemplation, help us to gain a better understanding of Mary, and we welcome every opportunity to know more about our Mother. The twelve writers of the outstanding book "Mary in the New Testament", which has served me well at several moments in my own writing of this book, say the following about Mary's silence:

> Luke's relative silence about Mary after Cana is surprising after we have shared and enjoyed his interest in her in the narrative of Jesus' first years. On the other hand, once we realise that Luke's interest in Mary was primarily directed to her as a symbol of the first believer, of Jesus' discipleship, we understand better this change in Luke's emphasis. While Jesus was a child, no other person outside his Mother could throw light on the discipleship; and Mary would come up again at some moments and even up to the end of the Church in the gathering of the first Christians. But in the narrative of Jesus' ministry the discipleship can be illustrated through a larger circle of Jesus' disciples, particularly the twelve. This accounts for the change of emphasis (p. 160).

This means to say that Mary has been presented,

in her person and in her attitude, as the ideal disciple at the beginning of the gospel. Later on, it becomes important to enlarge that area to other disciples, beginning with the twelve, into concentric circles of more and more disciples, and so the attention is turned towards them in the gospel narrative, to come back at the end to Mary in the Upper Room where Pentecost took place and the Church was born. "All these with one accord were constantly at prayer, together with a group of women, and Mary the mother of Jesus, and his brothers" (Acts 1:14).

Mary comes thus to be the disciple par excellence, present already at the dawn of redemption which she ushers in with her faith, her commitment, her listening to the word and her ready and unconditional following of it; and then present, too, when the resurrection has united the disciples again, the first group has been formed, the Holy Spirit comes upon them in power and joy, and the Church is born to gather all men and women as children of one common Mother.

After the celebrations at Cana, there is a brief mention of Mary in the sacred text, which it is good to recall. After winding up the narrative of the miracle with the phrase, "So Jesus performed at Cana in Galilee the first of the signs which revealed his glory and led his disciples to believe in him", John continues, "After this he went down to Capernaum with his mother, his brothers, and his disciples, and they stayed there a few days" (2:12). We feel joy in our heart when we imagine Jesus, already fully a man, walking together with Mary between neighbouring villages and spending time with her among friends. It is true that they travelled in a group with relatives and friends, but the pilgrim closeness of Mother and Son imprints itself on our imagination, our memory, and our love as an intimate scene that fills up landscapes of the soul with the cherished profiles along the routes of the gospel.

Mary keeps quiet. Her silence speaks out. Silence is God's own language. Holy things are beyond speech, and so our best way to refer to them is silence. Court manners in heavenly places are short speech and long silences. Jesus said it: "In your prayers do not go babbling on like the heathen, who imagine that the more they say the more likely they are to be heard. Do not imitate them, for your Father knows what your needs are before you ask him" (Matthew 6:7-8).

God fills our souls with his silence when he wants to regale us with his presence. Jesus' words in his preaching are brief, and it is in their briefness that they open up the spaces of our soul for us to make them our own, to embrace them, to assimilate them, to integrate them, applying to ourselves the repeated warning: "He who has ears to hear with, let him hear." Jesus, who is the eternal Word of the Father pronounced from all eternity, embodies in his

110

singularity all that the Father has to say as he expresses himself in the person of the Son and the Trinity with the Spirit, and so he is sparing of words that have to reflect on earth the one and ineffable essence of his person and his message. And those who understand him, imitate him.

Mary understood him. And so this is the lesson of Mary's silence too. She has heard, has understood, has answered, has said what she had to say, and now she knows, too, how to keep quiet and to wait, and to express only through her presence and her silence that she is there, that she accepts and understands and encourages and supports all that her Son does, while her quiet image represents in a profile of beauty and peace all the best we men and women can hope to be on this earth.

This does not mean that we are not to speak when circumstances demand that we should speak; of course we must speak, and we must even shout and raise our voices when life in our world leads us to denounce suffering and claim justice. But every action has to be based on reflection, and every word has to be conceived in silence. The words of Jesus and of Mary are full of strength because they both did much more than they spoke.

Here I want to point out, with all delicacy and all firmness, some abuses to which a well-meant but not well-advised devotion to Mary has led, which do

111

no honour to her and cause harm to the Church. I make this clear with an example. In a volume of alleged revelations of Mary, among the many such volumes pious souls present to me in my journeys to my own embarrassment and chagrin, are summed up the words Our Lady is supposed to have personally revealed to a certain devotee, which begin with the peremptory order, "Write about me!"; and then goes on the fill no less than ten volumes of more than a thousand pages each! This, in my opinion, does not become Mary. That is not her character, her style, herself. That is not Mary of Nazareth. Such a loquacity does not go with her, does not fit her image, is not true to the Gospel. And worse still are those exaggerations they put on her lips, the dire threats to sinful humankind, the setting up of herself as the one who will save us from the Father who only wants to punish us in his wrath, the insistence that we pray to her and build sanctuaries to her as the only remedy to all the evils of the world, and her assurance that all that will be well if we comply with her wishes. All that is out of place, out of good taste and against Christian theology.

Here are some unsavoury quotations from those supposed "revelations". In one of them Jesus is made to tell Mary: "You alone can change the Eternal Father's decrees for the punishment of humankind, because the Trinity will never be able to refuse anything to its Flower." In another she reviles all priests as "Apostates, Marxists, victims of Satan!" In yet another she promises that all these evils will be avoided only if "all faithful pray my Rosary to me, and build a Sanctuary dedicated to my cult." She even orders a tender child to undergo bodily penances to the shedding of blood. All this, and much more, does not fit a Mother, does not fit the lovely Maid of Nazareth, does not fit the Mother of Jesus and our own Mother as we know her from the gospels.

The Japanese Catholic writer Shusaku Endo became famous for his historical novel *Silence,* in which he describes the historical mission to Japan of the Jesuit Portuguese priest Sebastian Rodrigues with all the hardships it entailed at the time. In the novel there appears an episode grounded in history, in which Inoue, the magistrate, wants all Christians to apostatise, and in order to find out who are really Christian, orders them to step on a picture of Jesus. Whoever refuses to step on the picture of Jesus set on the floor, will be declared a Christian and will be summarily executed. The Christians consult Father Rodrigues, and he instructs them that, since the picture is only a piece of paper and Jesus knows well their faith and their good intention, and does not want them to die, Jesus would not mind them to step on the paper, and so they can do it with a good conscience. So the Christians present themselves before the magistrate for the test, and they step, one by one, as required by the authorities, on the picture of Jesus. But the wicked magistrate who was an apostate himself and knew well the ways of the Christians, tells them further: "That is not enough to prove that you are not Christian. You have stepped on the picture of Jesus; but you must now step on the picture of Mary," and places a picture of Our Lady on the floor. The Christians recoil and answer: "That we'll never do. We've managed, with sorrow, to step on the picture of Our Lord, but we'll never step on the picture of Our Lady." And they are condemned and executed. Father Rodrigues learns of the sad outcome and comments to himself: "Yes, they are martyrs for the faith. But is that really Christian faith?"

There are exaggerations in some attitudes, and these do the true faith no honour. With all due respect to those who defend the multiple and repeated apparitions of Our Lady, and with no less love for Mary and zeal for her glory as all of them surely have, I clearly express my opinion that those publications and communications, of which I've quoted a few and receive many, are unworthy of Mary, foreign to the Gospel, and do more harm that good to Mary's cult, to the Catholic Church and to the Gospel.

I deem it timely to quote here the conclusions with which the Jesuit priest Félix Moracho of Caracas in Venezuela, beloved friend and admired spiritual teacher, closes his outstanding book on Our Lady, "The Virgin Mary is Mary of Nazareth." The title of the final chapter is, "The Apparitions, the Church, and the Faith", and here is the text:

"I only note down here a few points of the doctrine of the Church that may help us to adopt a truly Christian position before the apparitions.

1. All that we humans need to know about God and our salvation has already been communicated to us fully and definitively in Christ. God does not do things by halves. Jesus is our only and definitive saviour. (Vatican Council II, Constitution *Dei Verbum,* 4.)

2. That communication or revelation from God to us is contained in Holy Scripture and in the Apostolic Tradition. *(Dei Verbum,* 7–9.)

3. This revelation has already been completed. We are not to look for new ways of salvation or original formulas for holiness. We can only grow in our understanding of the contents of the one and only revelation. The magisterium of the Church cannot increase that revelation and cannot recognise any new revelation that may demand the faith of the believers as Holy Scripture and the Apostolic Tradition do legitimately demand.

4. The magisterium of the Church, and only the magisterium has the right to interpret authentically the word of God, spoken or written, and the revelation contained in it. *(Dei Verbum,* 10.)

5. Surely we can set no limits to God. God can reveal himself or communicate with any person or persons by means of Mary. Such revelations will always be private, because the divine

115

revelation meant for all men and women was over with the apostles and what they transmitted to us. *(Dei Verbum,* 8.)

6. When the Church intervenes and recognises an "apparition", she does not impose, and cannot impose the obligation to believe in it in Christian faith, nor the obligation to believe the message of that apparition to be a divine message, not even the obligation to take that apparition as a divine fact.

7. This approbation of the Church (which is very rarely given) means only and exclusively that this fact has nothing against the faith and morals of the Catholic Church.

8. Christians keep their faith safe and intact when, acting according to their conscience, they do not believe, they do not give their assent to such apparitions, revelations or messages.

9. If all such apparitions would turn out to be false, the Catholic faith would not in any way be harmed. The content of the faith, the faith of the Church, does not depend on the continued "apparitions" or revelations. And our own faith, as persons and as a community, must not depend on them either.
(pp. 81–82.)

Thank you, dear friend and respected theologian, for the courage, the clarity and the truth of these declarations.

NEAR THE CROSS

"Near the cross on which Jesus hung, his Mother was standing."

It is to John that we owe this mention of Mary at the foot of the cross. He is the only evangelist to mention Mary, and to specify that she was near the cross. The other three evangelists mention only the other women, and they place them at a distance from the cross. Matthew says:

A number of women were also present, watching from a distance; they had followed Jesus from Galilee and looked after him. Among them were Mary of Magdala, Mary the mother of James and Joseph, and the mother of the sons of Zebedee (27: 55–56).

Luke himself, who has given so much importance

to Mary at the beginning of Jesus' life, does not mention her at the end. The fact that John does mention her, and does it in very explicit and relevant terms, has a special interest for us. For John, the cross-and-resurrection are two events fused into one, and that single moment, often announced and always expected, is the climax of the "hour" of Jesus onto which converge all the partial hours, all the moments of grace, all the callings of the Father, which now find their fulfilment and their meaning in the final sacrifice and the definitive glory that crown Jesus' mission on earth. "When I am lifted up from the earth I shall draw everyone to myself" (John 12:32). Mary's explicit presence at that moment is her definitive consecration as an essential figure in God's plan for the salvation of his people. Mary was the first to receive the Angel's message at the Annunciation, and is now the closest at the foot of the cross to accompany Jesus' redeeming death for the life of the world.

Another important significance of the stressing of Mary's presence at that moment of John's gospel is that for John that was the supreme moment when Jesus was coming closest to "his own", that is to his group, his disciples, his Church. "It was before the Passover festival, and Jesus knew that his hour had come and that he must leave this world and go to the Father. He had always loved his own who were in the world, and he loved them to the end" (13:1). This text, which is the introduction to the last meeting that will take Jesus to the culmination of his work on earth, mentions the "hour" and "his own", and the fact that Mary forms part of that group when they come to the cross, consecrates her as the closest ever to Jesus, the first among "his own", and now the main character in the Church that is born with the gathering of disciples that will remain for ever. Once again John's testimony and the tradition he represents grant Mary a special importance since the very beginnings of the first Christianity.

Mary, at the foot of the cross, suffers, and her suffering is an integral part of her life as a person in a hostile world, of her faith as the first believer in the people of God that continues its pilgrimage through deserts of poverty and pain, and of her motherhood over all of us men and women in our own sufferings, trials, and death. We have watched Mary along all her life in her joys that she shared with others to uplift hearts and lighten up lives, and now, in the last day of her Son's life, we see her suffer as no human being has ever suffered on earth, so that she will be able to accompany and to understand suffering humankind and lessen its sufferings too. Her sensitivity as a woman and her love as a mother are pierced by the close and direct sight of the acute and long-drawn torment her beloved Son is suffering at the hands of hardened mercenaries and in the presence of a crowd that sharpens its own cruelty by yielding to the worst instincts of the sinful human heart. "Let him come down from the cross, and we'll believe in him."

119

Mary's suffering deepens her life, enhances her maternity, brings her presence closer to us. We, men and women on earth, suffer much in our lives, and Mary's suffering brings her closer to us in our darkest moments, gives her the right to be by our side when we feel abandoned by all, makes her into our obvious refuge when we do not see light and do not find our way. She suffered more, and she went ahead. She stood, without fainting, without seeking relief and without uttering a complaint, as witness and victim, silent and eloquent, overcome by pain and full of fortitude for herself and for all of us who would later find support in her firmness, meaning in her faith, solace in her tears. With those simple words, "his Mother was near the cross, standing", John has given us more theology and more consolation than deep studies and long considerations. Mary is our Mother in suffering.

Maybe it is the very suffering of humankind that has prompted Christian piety to insist, in its representations and its devotions, on the image of Our Lady of Sorrows, on her sufferings, her anguish, her solitude, more often and with greater emphasis than on her joys and glory. Mary is the Mother of a suffering people, not only in personal trials and individual problems, but even more and deeper in social injustice and racial oppression; and so she takes upon herself those sufferings, denounces those injustices, and points the way of liberation, which passes through the resurrection of Jesus and postulates the union of all faithful Christians and all men and women of good will to build up consciences, awaken responsibilities, unite efforts, and restore equality, justice and love. Mary blesses very specially this movement our days are witnessing to redeem humankind, which gives us hopes and makes us desire to do all that we can to shorten sufferings, suppress injustices and straighten up the history of all peoples.

It is our privilege to live in times in which humankind has woken up to the cause of social justice, and it is our joy and our strength to know that in this most important and cherished task in our lives we have Mary as our model, our inspiration, and our Mother. She, standing by the cross, teaches us to understand that same cross, to embrace it when God's inscrutable designs take us to it as they took his own Son, and to avoid it when we meet false sufferings which are not dutiful crosses but avoidable evils in us and in others. Mary unites us to fight at every level, as persons and as institutions and as citizens of the world against whatever causes injustice, inequality, poverty, oppression, and suffering to any person, family, group or nation in any corner of our neighbourhood or in any region of the world. Mary is present by the cross to take us through it to the joy that had been hers before and that will be hers again for ever, and which she wishes to share with all of us with all her heart.

121

MOTHER OF US ALL

"Woman, this is your son."

John, in all his gospel, never refers to Mary by her name, but calls her always "the Mother of Jesus". And since everything in John has its meaning, we must also look here for the reason of his choice of words. It is possible that by always calling Mary "the Mother of Jesus", John wants to emphasise her maternity, thus preparing the link between Mary's personal maternity of Jesus and her universal maternity of all men and women when we come to see ourselves as brothers and sisters of Jesus. Mary, for John, is first and foremost the Mother, and he wants to settle that clearly in his Gospel through his own experience with her and his reflection on what Jesus and Mary meant to him and are meant to mean for all of us. Mary is Mother, and that, to John, is beautifully and justly her own personal name.

Now we hear again from the cross the term "woman" which we have already met, and which caused us some honest difficulty, while it also opened up for us new biblical horizons in seeing Mary's figure projected on to the whole of humankind. If we miss in that word the personal touch of human love, we find instead the broadening of Mary's love and motherhood to embrace all of us with the co-operation of her Son who prefers to call her "woman" and so to take us all to her, so that the children of Eve may now truly and fully become the children of Mary.

There is no doubt, knowing John's ways and symbols in his gospel, that every word Jesus utters on the cross has a transcendental reach that takes it far beyond the concrete circumstances that prompted it. Jesus' words have always had echoes of history and rings of eternity; and his last, few, brief words pronounced in the midst of his pain and agony as summary and testament of his life on earth have very specially a permanent ring and a universal meaning that makes them reach each one of us with a personal message and a final encouragement for our faith.

When Jesus forgives those who are nailing his hands and feet to the cross with ruthless nails, "because they do not know what they are doing," he is forgiving all of us when we hurt our brothers and sisters in their souls or their bodies with wounds that are to the Body of his Church what the nails in his body were to his own body on Good Friday.

When he is thirsty, he is first of all and with real anguish thirsty for water to relieve his loss of blood, his dried up throat which has not drunk anything since the farewell cup at his last supper, his discomfort at the heat of the sun over his naked body in the dust of midday; but then he is also thirsty with the thirst of his soul of which he had spoken all his life, "thirst for justice" (Matthew 5:6), thirst for "living water" (John 4:10), thirst to reach all men and women with his message, his redemption and his love, thirst for peace in the world and for equality in society, thirst for the Kingdom of God and its consummation in history.

When he tells the man on the other cross to his right who has asked him to remember him in his glory, "Today you will be with me in Paradise," he is in his mercy opening the gates of heaven to all those who look up to him and plead for mercy.

When he shouts, "My God, my God, why have you forsaken me?", he is lending us words of unheard-of clarity that we too may use them in our trials and depressions and loneliness, as he identifies himself with our sufferings and allows us to make his words our own.

When he proclaims, "It is accomplished!", he sums up, for himself and for us, the fulfilment of the mission his Father had entrusted him with here on earth, which is the beginning and promise of our own

124

missions from the Father who sends us "as he sent him."

When, finally, he utters his last cry that moved the centurion, "Father, into your hands I commit my spirit!", he affirms his final hope in the Father's love, which is our own definite hope in our lives, and the sound of our own voice in our death.

And so, when he, from the cross, points to his beloved disciple and tells Mary, "Woman, this is your son," Jesus is not only fulfilling his duty as a son to see to it that his Mother will have a home and support for the rest of her life when he will not be there to look after her, but, in those same words and through them, he is telling Mary that we all, who in our smallness and humility are all beloved disciples in his personal and universal love, are also her sons and her daughters, that we all are one family, that we love her as a Mother, and that she can count on us, as we count on her, for the life of the Church that is to prolong along ages and history, through all times and all lands, the life that Jesus lived for thirty-three years with her in Palestine.

Good Friday is the climax of history, centre of universes, focus of eternity. Every drop of blood on that mount is worth a redemption, every gesture is a prophecy, every word is sacred doctrine. In that moment of open perspectives and historical consequences, Mary is entrusted by her Son with the care of all her other children, that is, ourselves. It is

125

in the labour of this supreme mission that Mary gives us birth in grace, takes us to her bosom, makes us her own. From then on we'll be "sons in the Son", as the Fathers of the Church loved to say. Jesus, in his last farewell, has thought not only of his Mother, but of all of us too. His death, in truth, gives us life. We now have a Mother for ever.

FAREWELLS THAT UNITE

"This is your Mother."

I wrote my first literary composition when I was fourteen. It was published in the school magazine of the Jesuit school in Spain where I was a boarder. That was the magazine's issue after the Holy Week holidays, that is, at the beginning of the paschal season, and I wrote a very short piece in the style of the day which consisted in short sentences in different lines without any pretence to verse, but as a kind of rhythmical prose. The theme was prompted to me precisely by the seasonal moment in the liturgy; I gave it the title "This is your Mother", and this was the little piece that is still in my memory:

> Holy Week is just over,
> but it has left us a gift in passing,

a gift as only God can give.
He has given us his Mother as our Mother,
and we know what that means.
We now have love and care in our lives,
we have someone to rejoice when we rejoice
and to stand by us when we falter.
We have company,
we have help,
we have tenderness.
We have a Mother.
Thank you, Jesus.

That was not much of a literary masterpiece, and I must also recognise, too, that I was helped in his composition by the Spiritual Father of the school. But still, the effort was mine, and to see that little original piece of mine printed in the school magazine gave me great satisfaction, as it is proved by the fact that I remember it today after so many years. In that simple beginning I want to see now, as a humble projection in the symbolic style of John's gospel, a seed and a promise of all that with the passing of the years I would come to write and to publish abundantly in three languages. Everything began with Mary.

A short time after I arrived in India, an event took place that influenced me greatly and for quite a long time, and that in a most unexpected way. On November 1st 1950 Pope Pius XII proclaimed to the whole of Christendom the dógma of the Assumption of Our Lady into heaven. It was only a few months after my arrival in India, I was still struggling with the learning of English and with the courses in mathematics I was following for my degree in Madras University, new still to the place and the climate, freshly arrived from Spain, ignorant of customs and far still from friends and familiarity which would take time to come. Busy though I was with all this activity, I did come to know the news that the dogma was going to be proclaimed, but could not give the news much attention or any importance.

And then something strange happened. I repeat that I was as busy as I could be with my English and mathematics and Indian manners and Indian spices and the heat and the rains and the new friendships and the new customs and all that new universe which a young man of twenty-four is trying to understand and to assimilate with all the enthusiasm of having left his country and his family for Christ and wanting now to consecrate his whole life to serve in every way he could a new people he did not yet know but he was beginning to love from the heart.

And in the midst of all that turmoil and bewilderment and struggle, came all of a sudden a feeling that swept everything in my life with unexpected strength and power. It was a feeling of deep and tender devotion, of joy in prayer, of a constant sensation of walking on clouds, breathing ozone and contemplating sunrises at every corner, a tender love towards Mary far greater and deeper than any I had felt in all my life, a rejoicing with her joy, feeling glorious with her glory, and simply enjoying with all my being the plain certainty that she was, as indeed I had always known, body and soul in heaven, and that the Pope in Rome had proclaimed this truth with all his infallible authority, and the whole world was speaking about it, and Mary's name was on the lips of everyone, and this was a great day for everybody everywhere, and then also for me as it truly was. That blessed state lasted for months in my soul, and words fall short to describe the bit of heaven that was truly mine for all that period.

The bliss passed at length, but it left me wondering about the tide of feeling and believing that had swept over me with such a suddenness, such a strength, and such a duration. I take it now as part of that wave of Mary's blessing that thrilled its way through the whole of Christendom and that shook me as few experiences have ever done in my life. I saw it then, and see it now on recollection, as the true celebration organised in heaven and displayed on earth to honour Mary in her feast, which went beyond lights and canticles and sermons and treatises, and gave what only God can give, which is a sudden joy in one's heart, a familiarity in prayer, a personal feast in liturgy and Gospel as the one I put up for myself in between my studies of mathematics and my struggling with English. I know that Jesus wanted to celebrate his Mother's feast, and he distributed on that day an abundant quantity of Cana's wine, better, as it was said when it was first tasted, than all vintages in all ages and all vine-cellars.

I came later to learn some Sanskrit, the mother of all languages, at least all Indo-European languages, and there I came to know that the root for mother is *matru,* from where voices like *Mutter, madre, mother,* are derived in an almost universal pronunciation. One could think that, as the concept of "mother" is universal in its meaning of love and tenderness, so it is universal, too, in its spelling and its phonetics. All cultures celebrate the mother, and all religions revere her. We need to know and feel ourselves as sons and daughters, to know and feel that a woman, who is the crown of God's creation, loves us as her own, has given us our being, has looked after us with all the care, the delicacy and the sacrifice the human heart is capable of. We need to return again and again to our mother's lap, to the arms that always wait for us, to the warmth that reminds us of our origin. And in order that we may have a mother wherever and whenever we are, in body and in spirit, in tenderness and devotion, in permanent help and secure protection, in faith and reality for ever, Jesus has give us his own Mother in the most solemn moment of his life, when his words are his last will and his sacrifice is our redemption. "This is your Mother."

These blessed words, which have accompanied me for life, bring to my memory another event that enacted in my life something of what Jesus lived in his own life. I am twenty-four and am standing in Madrid airport together with a group of Jesuit companions eager to leave for India with the Gospel in our heart, resigned never to come back to our land and our families in those times in which the journey to mission lands was undertaken once and for all and there was no return for life. The farewell was till heaven. We would never meet again the friends we left in Spain, our families, our mothers. Air travel was not yet common, distances were long, and the parting was for ever. We knew the fact, we accepted it, we embraced it. It was the supreme sacrifice, both on our side and on the side of our most dear ones, but it was part of our calling, and so it was willingly undertaken on all sides. The thrill of the spiritual adventure dulled somehow the feeling of pain at the parting moment, but the merciless departure was nevertheless a moment of trauma in the midst of all the blessings of the mission.

I now see in the eye of my mind my own mother, with a face that photographs of that day have preserved for me and that tear apart my soul in searing pain even now as I see them. I see that pale face, white, empty, elongated like a single tear, silent in its nameless suffering. That figure, standing also by her own cross with all the suffering of the world in her mother's heart. She is looking at me with the feeling that she will never see me again. I, also, cannot think of anything to say.

At that moment, words I had not thought of, I had not prepared in any way since nothing can be prepared for moments which can only be lived in their intensity with all their tenderness and all their ruthlessness, words wholly spontaneous and unexpected came to my lips and I heard myself telling my mother what I had not imagined I would be telling her. And these were the words: "See, mummy, I am leaving now, and it is not probable that we will ever meet again. You have looked after me very well in all my life since the day I was born, and even more since daddy died and you became a widow and you had to fight to bring up my brother and me. You did it very well, you gave us a good education, and that is how I have come to this moment that takes me to a chosen work as a privileged soul. I have not been able to do anything for you, mummy, and much less will I be able to do anything from now on. I shall not be able to look after you, and no one is here to whom I could entrust you. But I know Jesus, I can certainly entrust you to his care. He also had a Mother and he took care to leave her settled when he was leaving her from the cross. That is why now I tell Jesus, and I know he will take my request seriously, 'Look, Jesus, this is your mother. You look after her now.' He'll look after you better than I could do."

We said nothing more. We embraced and kissed for the last time, and we parted. I'd thought I would still be able to see her from inside the plane through the window, as there were no restrictions in those first days of commercial flights and well-wishers could come right up to a rail close to the plane. But I could not see her. Maybe my tears didn't let me see. The flight had its first stop in Rome, and the new impressions soon erased the last emotions. It is a fact that in all farewells the one who stays back suffers more than the one who departs.

Many years have passed since that date. The ways of the world changed, facility of travel increased, movements and visits became normal, and I could meet my mother again and renew the sacred bonds of family and birth. When, with age, the time came for me to retire from teaching, and for her to need someone by her side for company and care in her old age, I could go and spend long periods by her side, and finally do something for her who had done so much for me. When I would ask her in those days, "How are you, mother?" her answer was always the same: "With you very well, my son." When she died in my arms at 101 years of age, I was happy to have been of use to her when she most needed help, and she was grateful to have had in her last days my company which she had missed so long. Jesus knows how to carry out responsibly the work we lovingly entrust to him.

A SPECIAL WAY OF THE CROSS

"The disciple took her into her home."

In the small church of a remote village an old woman used to pray the Way of the Cross every day. She would devotedly go from one station to another in the fourteen images, stop in front of each, and say the corresponding prayers she knew by heart from the long repetition. And once she had completed the fourteen stations, she went again from one to another, this time in the opposite direction, beginning with the last and ending at the first, and then, after a long look at the tabernacle and a slow genuflexion, she would cross herself with holy water and leave the church. The parish priest observed her daily prayer, and one day he could not keep back his curiosity and asked her delicately: "Granny, I see every day how you go through the Way of the Cross with all devotion, but I don't understand why you make it twice, once when going and once when coming. Could you explain to me why you do that?" The old woman explained: "First I do the Way of the Cross as it is, accompanying Jesus in his sufferings; and then I do it the other way, accompanying Mary in her recollection of those same sufferings as she comes back with John to go to his house."

That is Mary's own Way of the Cross. The old woman understood it well, as she too was woman and mother who in her long life must have walked ways of thorns too, and knew how one felt when revisiting in memory the places where one had suffered in the flesh. In biblical numerology, fourteen is twice seven, and seven is the sacred number that straddles the Bible from the seven days of creation and the Sabbath rest on the seventh day to the seven churches of the Apocalypse and the seven sacraments of our Christian life. Doubling the number means underlining the pain Jesus and Mary suffered for us in the hours of the passion. All our memory and accompaniment and compassion cannot equal the weight of suffering that made up our redemption. Catholic tradition has acknowledged that suffering and has expressed it in images and songs and processions and prayers, and this tradition is a genuine and sincere manifestation of all that we, children of Mary, feel at the memory of all that our Mother suffered for us.

Now Mary does not suffer any more. Against the claims of some "apparitions" that present Mary in anguish and sorrow in heaven for our sins on earth, Mary does not suffer now, as Jesus does not suffer after his resurrection and ascension to his Father's side. The true approach to human suffering now is the one given by St. Paul already in his time with his authentic and pointed theology. The passion of Jesus is over, but the sufferings of the human race continue, and so in a way that passion still goes on in us, who in all humility and faith unite our actual sufferings to his past ones to complete Jesus' work as Paul says:

> It is now my joy to suffer for you; for the sake of Christ's body, the Church, I am completing what still remains for Christ to suffer in my own person. I became a servant of the Church by virtue of the task assigned to me by God for your benefit; to put God's word into full effect, that secret purpose hidden for long ages and through many generations, but now disclosed to God's people. To them he has chosen to make known what a wealth of glory is offered to the Gentiles in this secret purpose; Christ in you, the hope of glory. He it is whom we proclaim. We teach everyone and instruct everyone in all the ways of wisdom, so as to present each one of you as a mature member of Christ's body. To this end I am toiling strenuously with all the energy and power of Christ at work in me (Colossians 1:24-29).

Beautiful Pauline text that sheds light over our own situation and at the same time gives us strength and purpose to carry out the mission that, in humble proportion, is also our own. Jesus – and Mary with him – already inhabits the glory of heaven; but his Way of the Cross continues here on earth. The weight of its fourteen stations is heavy upon humankind in hunger and poverty, in injustice and oppression, in sickness and death. And it is we who are called to take upon ourselves that suffering, face that oppression, denounce that injustice and think and speak and do all that we can in our utmost effort to relieve that suffering, to level out that inequality, to put an end to the corruption that eats up our society, and obtain a just order with peace and freedom for all upon earth.

This is the meaning of the Gospel in our lives, the mission which, like Paul, we accept with joy, even in the midst of our own sufferings, to show to the world the riches of the mystery of our faith, which is none other than Christ himself in all men and women as our "hope of glory" in an unsurpassable expression of human greatness and divine faith. We are the heirs to the passion of Christ, to be then the heirs of his glory too; and the same holds good of our relationship to Mary's sufferings on earth: we make now our own all that she suffered in her earthly life, and together with that we do all we can to diminish the sufferings of all peoples and to redeem our society today. The

138

best way for us to show our love to Mary and to venerate her is to help those who suffer in body and in mind, to make that mission our own and so to strive for the redemption and freedom of humankind from want.

Mary knew sufferings in her life, even before the agony of Good Friday, and she also knew of other people's sufferings in her time and in her vicinity; and those sufferings affected also her Mother's heart and led her to help and comfort those who suffered and were within her reach in word and in action. Without inventing fictitious situations or imagining artificial happenings, but only following up some brief hints we find in the gospels themselves, we can respectfully trace down a few instances of sufferings of others which Mary heard about in her life and must have made her own. Such considerations can help us to delve deeper into Mary's own feelings, and consequently to react better when we learn of other people's sufferings.

Mary did not directly know about the killing of the Innocents in Bethlehem after the birth of her Son and the visit of the Magi, because the Angel warned Joseph in anticipation to escape in time, and mentioned only the necessary point that "Herod is going to search for the child to kill him." And on their return from Egypt, after another warning to Joseph in his dream, they went straight to Nazareth without Mary ever going back to Bethlehem so far as we

139

know. But there is still the possibility that from mouth to mouth and from village to village news would travel, even more so in those days when the grapevine was the chief means of communication, and Mary could hear in her day reports of the event that had shaken the whole land:

> When Herod realised that the Magi had tricked him he flew into a rage, and gave orders for the massacre of all the boys aged two years or under, in Bethlehem and throughout the whole district, in accordance with the time he had ascertained from the Magi. So the words spoken through Jeremiah the prophet were fulfilled: 'A voice was heard in Rama, sobbing in bitter grief; it was Rachel weeping for her children, and refusing to be comforted, because they were no more' (Matthew 2:16–18).

Another bit of news did reach Nazareth through its permanent connection with Jerusalem in business and goods and caravans and pilgrimages, and that was the appearance of a new prophet, John the Baptist, near the waters of the river Jordan. Together with descriptions of his person and his baptism, rumours also must have reached Nazareth about his preaching and his open denunciation of crime and wrongdoing, and of the worst sin of society in those days, as it continues to be in ours, that is, inequality and injustice. This is what people said:

The people asked him [John the Baptist], 'Then what are we to do?' He replied, 'Whoever has two shirts must share with him who has none, and whoever has food must do the same.' Among those who came to be baptised were tax-collectors, and they said to him, 'Teacher, what are we to do?' He told them, 'Exact no more than the assessment.' Some soldiers also asked him, 'And what of us?' To them he said, 'No bullying; no blackmail; make do with your pay!' (Luke 3:10–14).

Here are the germs of injustice and inequality in any society, and Mary heard about it in Nazareth, as Jesus heard it when he left Nazareth and went directly to the Jordan to be baptised by John. Humankind has always been the same. Shopkeepers who overcharge, authorities who abuse their power, officials who blackmail and oppress the downtrodden. And the poor people who suffer and have no defence before those who attack them and enslave them from above. This is the suffering Mary underwent in herself and saw around herself all her life. That was the life of the lowly people where she belonged.

We can imagine Mary's suffering when another sad news reached Nazareth, swift with the trauma of the crime and hushed up with the fear of the mighty. That was the cruel death, at the hands of a brutal and whimsical king, of the great prophet who had raised the hopes of Israel and had prepared the way for her own Son: John the Baptist. "Then John's disciples came and took away the body, and buried it; and they went and told Jesus." (Matthew 14:12) Mary also came to know and grieved over it. The child who had stirred with joy in Elisabeth's womb when Mary had visited her, died now beheaded in a dark dungeon. Her own family life was full of sorrows for Mary too.

A moment of sharp pain and agony did come to Mary in that sudden outburst of jealousy and madness that threatened Jesus' life at the beginning of his public life and in his own village of Nazareth on a Sabbath day. It all began well, but after all in the synagogue had admired his words, full of wisdom and eloquence, they felt themselves provoked by Jesus' saying that "no prophet is recognised in his own country" and rushed forward to kill him while Mary, in all surety, was among the Sabbath congregation at the synagogue. This is the dramatic event that Mary lived in full that ominous day:

> He began to address them: 'Today,' he said, 'in your hearing this text [of the prophet Isaiah] has come true.' There was general approval; they were astonished that words of such grace should fall from his lips. 'Is not this Joseph's son?' they asked. Then Jesus said, 'No doubt you will quote to me the proverb, "Physician, heal yourself" and say, "We have heard of all your doings at Capernaum; do the same here in your own home town".' 'Truly I tell you', he went on: 'no prophet

is recognised in his own country. There were indeed many widows in Israel in Elijah's time, when for three years and a half the skies never opened, and famine lay hard over the whole country; yet it was to none of these that Elijah was sent, but to a widow at Sarepta in the territory of Sidon. Again, in the time of the prophet Elisha there were many lepers in Israel, and not one of them was healed, but only Naaman, the Syrian.' These words roused the whole congregation to fury; they leapt up, drove him out of the town, and took him to the brow of the hill on which it was built, meaning to hurl him over the edge. But he walked straight through the whole crowd and went away (Luke 4:21–30).

In Nazareth they still show a sharp height in the land from which they had meant to throw Jesus to his death below, and another farther mount, on which, according to tradition, Mary stood horrified while she watched the whole scene till she could breathe relief at seeing her Son escape safe. The horror of that scene must have remained imprinted in her mother's heart till the end of her days.

Mary knew also of another and more subtle oppression, as it was done in the name of religion, of which were guilty the religious authorities of the time who manipulated the innocent consciences of simple people with threats and impositions beyond all reason or justice. Mary learned about that when someone told her what Jesus himself had told those religious leaders to their faces, with a clarity and a courage that already foretold in sad prophecy the fatal end to which that frontal opposition would lead. Jesus had said before all the people:

> The scribes and Pharisees make up heavy loads and pile them on the shoulders of others, but will not themselves lift a finger to ease the burden.

> Alas for you, scribes and Pharisees, hypocrites! You shut the door of the kingdom of Heaven in people's faces; you do not enter yourselves, and when others try to enter, you stop them.

> O Jerusalem, Jerusalem, city that murders the prophets and stones the messengers sent to her! How often have I longed to gather your children, as a hen gathers her brood under her wings; but you would not let me. Look! There is your temple, forsaken by God and laid waste'
> (Matthew 23: 4, 13, 37).

Whatever hurt Jesus, hurt Mary too. The ruin of Jerusalem, the hypocrisy of religious authorities, the oppression of consciences by imposing burdens they themselves could not bear. This oppression of consciences with burdens impossible to bear, laws impossible to keep, and the complex of guilt for not measuring up to the standards imposed, is the most painful oppression of all times, and the faithful people suffer under it.

144

Mary heard also, in the daily exchanges between women by the well, or the harmless gossip among neighbours in the street, news or rumours of events in the land, far and near, of political changes or natural disasters that then as always affected people's lives and were eagerly commented in village circles. Many must such occasions have been, about which we shall never know, but there are two whose mention found its way into the gospels, two pieces of news that reached Jesus' ears, and undoubtedly also Mary's. This is how the gospel tells them:

> At that time some people came and told him [Jesus] about the Galileans whose blood Pilate had mixed with their sacrifices. He answered them: 'Do you suppose that, because these Galileans suffered this fate, they must have been greater sinners than anyone else in Galilee? No, I tell you; but unless you repent, you will all of you come to the same end.

> Or the eighteen people who were killed when the tower fell on them at Siloam – do you imagine they must have been more guilty than all the other people living in Jerusalem? No, I tell you; but unless you repent, you will all come to an end like theirs' (Luke 13:1–5).

This unexpected passage presents us, in the times and in the knowledge of Jesus, the two great sources of human suffering today as always: political oppression and natural disasters. We know about those

145

two calamities nothing more than what the gospel tells us here, but to me it is very significant and very instructive that we should be told about them at all, as they alert us and awaken our consciences to the closest and greatest causes of social and family suffering. The Roman governor orders the slaughter of a group of Galileans who had gone with their offerings to the temple; and a tower suddenly collapses and kills with its falling debris eighteen workers at Siloam. A tyrannical order from a political despot and a labour accident. It would seem we are reading today's news in the paper. And these are news that reached Jesus through the media of his day, and must have reached Mary through the same channels too. Humankind's sufferings continue.

After this brief survey of calamities and sufferings that are told in the gospels and that as such were known to Jesus and to Mary with him, it is for us now, in the spirit in which Paul "completed in his flesh what still remained for Christ to suffer", to complete also now and carry on with the redeeming action of Jesus and Mary before natural disasters or human crimes, to feel them in ourselves with all the closeness of inner brotherhood, to lament them as though they touched us personally, to help those who suffer in every way we can and with all the means at our disposal, and to fight and denounce and proclaim and organise campaigns and enlighten consciences to allay suffering, defeat injustice, free the oppressed, reconcile enemies, establish equality, renew love in the world.

146

The tower fell at Siloam, and the Galileans were killed by Pilate. I have seen lands made desolate by war, by earthquakes, by volcanoes, by storms that have created a havoc of poverty and of pain. I have seen and heard about abuses and oppressions and corruption and violence as those denounced by John the Baptist in the society in which he lived, and endured by him in his own flesh. I have felt and continue to feel the trauma of the oppression of consciences when norms are imposed, voices are silenced, protests are squashed, prophets are exiled. I have felt, perhaps more than anything else, the death of children whom I have not seen in reality but whose helpless images I have watched on the TV screen, brothers and sisters of the children of Bethlehem, with innocence on their faces and the whole world in their wide open eyes, with empty bodies and lifeless hands, with the whole promise of life written on their large foreheads and all the sadness of death hanging from their bare skeleton beneath their skin.

And here is where I see the real cult of Mary, the continuation of her presence, the devotion of her people. She is Mother, and as such she desires the welfare of all her sons and daughters, the more so for their suffering being the greater; and we now aim at continuing her presence with our responsibility, our care and our action for the weakest ones among our brothers and sisters. This is the meaning of going now through the Way of the Cross backwards with Mary on our way home. We want to identify in our surroundings the situations of want and suffering similar to those she knew and felt, and do then with our compassion and our action all we can as individuals and as organisations in order to make effective on earth the redemption that is already sanctioned in heaven.

148

JOY FOR EVER

"Rejoice, Queen of heaven!"

The word that started it all at the beginning, comes now again at the end. "Rejoice!" This is Mary's word par excellence, the one we use in our prayers to her, "Hail Mary!", "Hail, Holy Queen!", and "Hail, Queen of Heaven!" during paschal time in place of the *"Angelus"*. Here translations veil the real meaning of the word "hail", which in the original Greek of Luke's gospel in the narrative of the Archangel Gabriel's salutation is *jaire,* which literally means "rejoice!". In Latin this was translated as *"Ave"*, which is a word of greeting, and behind these vicissitudes lies a little biblical controversy which it will be interesting to disclose.

Jaire in Greek means first of all "rejoice!" as I have just said, since it is the imperative tense of the verb *jairo* which means "to rejoice". But it is also true that the word was also used as a common greeting when persons met on the street, like a "Hello!" or even a more informal "Hi!", and also as a way to begin or to end a letter. And here scholars are divided in our case. Some believe that the *jaire* of the Angel to Mary is a simple salutation without any special reference to joy, while others defend that the word maintains its original meaning of joy on the lips of the Angel. Stanislaus Lyonnet, biblical scholar and sharp interpreter, defends the latter interpretation both with his great personal authority and with his technical arguments. He shows, for instance, that in context reflecting the Semitic language Luke uses the Greek word *eirene* (which is "peace" in English and *shalom* in Hebrew) instead of *jaire* as an ordinary greeting (as, for instance, in 10:5 and 24:37), and therefore, when using *jaire* for Mary in the Annunciation which is a typical Semitic context, the Angel means clearly "rejoice!", and not a plain "greetings!", for which Luke would have used *eirene*.

Stanislaus Lyonnet has always been one of my favourite interpreters of the bible ever since I discovered his incomparable commentary of Paul's Epistle to the Romans and of the term "justice of God" in it. That is why I like to let myself be convinced by his arguments, particularly here when they coincide with my own sense of chivalry and love for Mary, which makes me feel much happier if I hear the

150

Angel tell Mary "Rejoice!", than if he were saying a plain, "Hi!".

So the word of the Angel to Mary, "Rejoice!", comes now back from our own lips as we announce to her in the haste of the morning of Easter Sunday the joy and the glory of the risen Christ and we tell her in our cherished prayer, "Hail, Queen of Heaven! Alleluia!" Mary's waiting for that word was brief, painful though it was. The Saturday of grief between the cross and the open tomb was the deepest solitude a human soul can experience on earth. But if Mary was the one who suffered most in those dark hours, she was also the first to be consoled by her risen Son in his morning of glory. My father St. Ignatius allows himself a moment of dry humour and a gesture of the errant knight in defence of his honoured Lady, when in his Spiritual Exercises, which do not otherwise shine for any literary or imaginative style, says when he comes to the apparitions of the risen Christ:

> About the resurrection of Christ our Lord and his first apparition. First point: He appeared to Our Lady, which fact, although it is not mentioned in the Scriptures, is taken for granted when it is said that he appeared to many others, because the Scriptures suppose that we have understanding, as it is written, 'Are you, too, still without understanding?', Matthew 15:16.

It is even possible that Mary's solitude lasted even less than we have calculated. Our dean of dogmatic

151

theology in the seminary liked to ask as this question, not without a smile of theological mischief on his face: "When did Jesus rise from the dead? Give me the day and the hour." And the answer he expected was, "Jesus rose from the dead on Good Friday at 3 o'clock in the afternoon." The resurrection of Jesus is the acceptance of his life, his offering, and his death on the part of the Father, and this takes place instantly the moment Jesus' sacrifice is consummated with his death on the cross. This is the clear concept John expresses in his gospel and Paul in his letters. The "being lifted up" of Jesus is for John the same movement that takes Jesus to be raised up on the cross, and taken up to his Father's embrace in heaven, and so death-resurrection and passion-glory are two inseparable movements that crown Jesus' life on earth and seal his eternity in heaven.

For Paul, Jesus "was given up to death for our misdeeds, and raised to life for our justification" (Romans 4:25), and these two phrases are the parallel expression of one and the same reality which is simultaneous and indivisible in itself. The redemption of our sins is our justification, as the death of Jesus is already his resurrection. The events of the last hours in Jesus' life are so dense that we do well to space them out and distinguish them in our contemplation and our celebration to venerate them in greater detail along prayers and vigils and processions and traditions, and so we do from time immemorial with true faith and timely devotion. But the theological reality is one and indivisible, and we feel happy to know it and to celebrate it accordingly. The theologian Raniero Cantalamessa, in his book, "Mary, Mirror of the Church", adds a historical testimony to this theological consideration:

> Under this light, the fact that the fourth gospel does not mention the risen Christ's apparition to Mary ceases to be important or strange. The women discovered Christ's resurrection at dawn on the third day, but Mary discovered it even earlier, as the resurrection dawned from the cross itself, when truly 'it was still dark'.

> We even have a historical confirmation of what I've just said, namely that for John the scene at Calvary includes already, if taken in its completeness, the resurrection of Christ. It is known that the Churches of Asia Minor, founded or presided over by John, celebrated Easter on the 14th Nisan, that is, on the anniversary day of the death of Christ, not three days later as it was done in the rest of the Churches that celebrated the Pasch on Sunday. And, from the texts we possess, we also know that in the liturgy of those Churches for that day, they did not commemorate the death of Christ only, but also and in the same way, his victory and resurrection.

> Thus John, presenting to us Mary as he does at the foot of the cross, places her at the very heart

of the paschal mystery. She was present, not only at the falling and death of her Son, but also at his raising and his glorification. 'We have seen his glory', exclaims John in his prologue, and he then refers to his glory on the cross. And Mary can say the same. She too has seen his glory, new and different from any other kind of glory that could be imagined by human thinking. She has seen 'the glory of God' which is eternal love (p. 116).

Mary is now in possession of the overflowing joy to know in its fullness the eternal glory of her beloved Son, and she now keeps in her heart that sacred intimacy, that sacramental tenderness, that feminine delicacy, that universal motherhood that make her for us all, now and for ever in eternity, for her own rejoicing and our unending bliss, the woman "blessed among women".

"Rejoice, Queen of Heaven!"

EVERYTHING HAS ITS TIME

"Together with Mary, the Mother of Jesus."

Years ago I wanted to write a book on Mary. And I could not do it. It was a strange experience. I had carefully prepared the best conditions and circumstances for the work; I had chosen the month of February, the most pleasant for me in India, as the little cold that can be experienced in my region is already over by January, and the heat that will rule over the rest of the year does not settle till March. I kept the whole of the month free. I wrote beforehand all the articles I had to publish in several newspapers and magazines during the month; I prepared all the mathematics classes I had to give during that period so that a quick look at my notes each day would be enough for the actual task, and so I kept the whole month entirely free in time and energy, fully to concentrate all my strength on the writing of the book.

I had also collected all my notes about Mary, I had the full idea of the book in my mind; I had prepared a detailed sketch, had filed all the quotations in order, had typed the titles of the chapters, and was looking forward with all enthusiasm and zest to the writing of that book about Mary when I had just written and published in the Gujarati language a book on the Sacred Heart of Jesus, another on the parables of the Gospel, and a third one on the Sermon on the Mount, and this was to follow now. I had promised myself this would be the best book of my life, and I relied on Mary's help and on Jesus' help too, which I had insistently requested for this book in honour of his Mother and mine.

I even did something special, and a little out of the way given the kind of life I was leading at the time. I was living as a wandering guest, begging for hospitality from house to house in simple neighbourhoods among Hindu families. I usually stayed for a week at each house, but on that occasion and with the aim of this book in mind, I asked a family to house me for a full month so that I would need not change houses with all the distraction and interruption that would entail when I wanted full concentration on this work. They agreed, I sat down on the floor in a corner of the main room of the house, took up paper and pencil and invoked the assistance of the patron saint of that street whose name was *Jadav Bhagatni Pole,* or "The Cul-de-sac of Saint Jadav", and got ready to begin.

I wanted a good beginning for my book, but I could not find the phrase. Never mind. I'm used to the goings and comings of inspiration, and I know how to wait for the subtle wave that moves the hand and the pen when ideas become words and thought becomes text. But the wave was not coming. The whole morning went blank. And it was a special morning at that. It was February 1st, the liturgical eve of the feast of the Presentation, when Mary went to the Temple for her own ritual purification after giving birth to Jesus, and for the official presentation of Jesus in the same Temple. Beautiful feast, enhanced by the canticle of Simeon and the caresses bestowed on the Child by Anna, aged eighty-four, daughter of Phanuel of the tribe of Asher. All lovely and inspiring thoughts. But not a word from my pen.

I took my lunch, mounted my bicycle, and went to the College to meet my classes, to see my companions and to celebrate the Eucharist as I did every day, and then I cycled back to the place which was my house for the month, to take supper at once with the family that kept me, and then settle down to my writing in the remaining hours of the day. But nothing came out either. And so the next day. And the next. And the next. Literary drought.

I felt it, but I was not worried. I knew the moment would come. It had happened to me before, though never quite so long to come. Writing has its ups and downs, its inspiration and its silences, and I

157

knew it and waited and tried and kept trying. I prayed harder, I struggled longer, I waited and waited. But no progress. The precious month I had so zealously kept intact for the chosen work was passing away... and hardly a word. Some days I still managed to literally push the pen along the paper and make it write something, but what I wrote was not worth even being read again. I tore down pages and began again. Nothing came out. If these desolate pages have succeeded in giving some idea of the mental despair caused by hours and hours spent uselessly before a blank page without writing a word, it will have achieved it purpose. I got fed up. I turned to Jesus and told him familiarly:

Look here, Jesus. You are to blame here. I thought you would be at least as interested as I am in seeing a good book about your Mother published in the Gujarati language. You know that I write creditably and they have given me prizes for that too; and as for this book you also know I was determined to make it the best of all the books I've ever written. And it simply is not coming out. And I can do no more. The month I allotted to it is already coming to an end, and I have to turn again to my literary commitments and my classes and my other works. So, I reluctantly have to give up, and the book will remain unwritten. Kindly explain that to our Mother.

I closed down the file with all the papers I had

prepared for the writing of the book, and put it away. I remained sad and empty. The next day I took another theme for one of my usual articles in the press, and I wrote normally. But it was too late to start on the book again, and anyway I was not in the mood. I never wrote that book.

Today I think I know why all that happened. One must give God time, even years, for his intentions somehow to show up. Putting it simply, if I had written that book then, I would not be writing this one now. And this one is, humbly, better that the old one would have been, and in a language that will reach more readers. I am now better prepared, I know more about Mary, I have lived longer under her mantle, I know life better and I have seen it now, besides India, in Spain and Latin America where Mary is a vital part of life of persons and countries, and as such teaches us the importance of her presence and the prudence to be had before excesses as I have indicated in its place. This book has been better written now than if it had been written in "The Cul-de-sac of Saint Jadav", which for me turned out truly to be in its true sense a "cul-de-sac" as I literally could not get out of it. I finally left the street, and left the project. And now I feel happy to have written this book, and thus having taken out the thorn that had remained in my flesh since then.

And maybe Jesus wanted to teach me, too, that this book was not entirely mine; that is, that the

159

menial work in it would be mine, but that the book was about his Mother, and so he wanted to show me that the inspiration had to come from him, the ideas from him, the time from him. Something of this I want humbly to think has happened, and that thought gives me happiness too.

The last mention Luke makes of Mary, already in his second book of the "Acts", places her in the Upper Room where the last events of the life of Christ had taken place and the first events of the life of the Church were taking place now. The apostles were there at prayer with a few women too who had followed Jesus in his public life, all of them "together with Mary, the Mother of Jesus" (Acts 1:14). That is the best thought to leave us with. Mary was there. And that tells it all. Wherever she is, there will be peace and love and union and prayer. And there will be the Holy Spirit coming down on all with wind and sound and tongues of fire to give us life and faith and joy and zeal in receiving God's grace in our hearts and desiring at once to share it with others. Mary was there. That is the blessing of our lives, the secret of our joy, the strength of our faith. In Mary we have a Mother, and in that heavenly, earthly, loving, caring, thoughtful and powerful Mother we go forth in life cheerful and happy.

Hail Mary, full of grace!